Lancastrians and Yorkists: The Wars of the Roses

David R. Cook

LONGMAN
London and New York

PEARSON EDUCATION LIMITED
Edinburgh Gate, Harlow
Essex CM20 2JE, England
and Associated Companies throughout the World.

Visit us on the World Wide Web at:
http://www.pearsoneduc.com

First published 1984

ISBN 0 582 35384 X

Set in 10/11pt. Baskerville, Linotron 202

Printed and bound by Antony Rowe Ltd, Eastbourne
Transferred to digital print on demand, 2005

British Library Cataloguing in Publication Data

Cook, David R.
Lancastrians and Yorkists. – (Seminar studies in history)
1. Great Britain – History – Wars of the Roses, 1455–1485
I. Title II. Series
942.04 DA250
ISBN 0–582–35384–X

Library of Congress Cataloging in Publication Data

Cook, David R.
Lancastrians and Yorkists.
(Seminar studies in history)

Bibliography: p.
Includes index.
1. Great Britain – History – Wars of the Roses, 1455–1485. I. Title. II. Series.
DA250.C67 1983 942.04 83–9387
ISBN 0–582–35384–X

Contents

Acknowledgements

We are grateful to the following for permission to reproduce copyright material:

Associated Book Publishers Ltd for extracts from *English Historical Documents* Vol IV edited by A. R. Myers published by Methuen; Oxford University Press for extracts from *The Usurpation of Richard III* edited by C. A. J. Armstrong 2nd Edition (c) Oxford University Press 1969.

Seminar Studies in History

Founding Editor: Patrick Richardson

Introduction

The Seminar Studies series was conceived by Patrick Richardson, whose experience of teaching history persuaded him of the need for something more substantial than a textbook chapter but less formidable than the specialised full-length academic work. He was also convinced that such studies, although limited in length, should provide an up-to-date and authoritative introduction to the topic under discussion as well as a selection of relevant documents and a comprehensive bibliography.

Patrick Richardson died in 1979, but by that time the Seminar Studies series was firmly established, and it continues to fulfil the role he intended for it. This book, like others in the series, is therefore a living tribute to a gifted and original teacher.

Note on the System of References:
A bold number in round brackets (**5**) in the text refers the reader to the corresponding entry in the Bibliography section at the end of the book. A bold number in square brackets, preceded by 'doc' [**doc. 6**] refers the reader to the corresponding item in the section of Documents, which follows the main text.

Part One: The Background

Fifteenth-Century England

The Lancastrian war in France 1415–1453

> Nor, indeed , is evidence to be found in the chronicles or annals of kings of which our long history makes mention, that any king of England ever achieved so much in so short a time and returned home with so great and so glorious a triumph.
>
> *Gesta Henrici Quinti* (**5**), pp. 100–101

The reign of Henry V (1413–1422) witnessed a level of achievement beyond all contemporary expectations. After his accession, Henry immediately set about reviving the military glories of his great-grandfather, Edward III. He was fortunate in the timing of his claim to the French throne as France was in turmoil due to the insanity of Charles VI. Henry invaded France in 1415. The campaign began with the successful siege of Harfleur and culminated in the great English victory at Agincourt (St Crispin's Day, 25 October 1415). It made King Henry a national hero.

However, the strain on the country's military and financial resources was already apparent. Henry was unable to follow up his triumphs of 1415 for two years. He then systematically conquered Lower Normandy. The campaign of 1417–1419 ended in the successful six-month siege of Rouen. Henry's triumph in France, which led to the capture of Paris, was sealed by the murder of Duke John the Fearless of Burgundy by the supporters of the Dauphin on the bridge at Montereau in September 1419. The Burgundians now became the firm allies of the English and the new Duke, Philip the Good, negotiated the Treaty of Troyes (May 1420) with Henry V. The English King was made heir to the French throne and was to marry the daughter of Charles VI. The Dauphin, now beleaguered and penniless in Bourges, was disinherited. It seemed as if all France lay at Henry's feet, but he had less than three years to live, and Troyes was not to be the final triumph, only a step in that direction.

Henry has been described as 'the greatest man that ever ruled

England', but in the context of the fifteenth century it is very difficult not to view him as an 'able but shortsighted adventurer' (**47**, p. 133). Even if he had lived, it is doubtful whether Henry could ever have firmly established the Lancastrian dynasty in France. The spirit of resistance, albeit somewhat dimmed, still shone in many areas of France. In England, on the contrary, there were definite signs of war-weariness. Henry was hard pressed for both men and money in the last years of his reign. Parliament had readily granted taxation in a first flush of enthusiasm for the war, but by the early 1420s the Commons were growing increasingly reluctant. Loans postponed the inevitable crisis, but as debts mounted so creditors became ever more wary.

Yet the Lancastrian empire survived the death of its creator in August 1422. On his death-bed, Henry designated his very able brother John, Duke of Bedford, as Regent in France. Bedford was able to maintain the vital Burgundian alliance and make steady military progress. The French were defeated at Cravant in July 1423 and again at Verneuil in August 1424. By the end of 1425 Maine and parts of Anjou were in English hands. Three years later the Earl of Salisbury, against the advice of Bedford, decided to seize a bridgehead over the Loire and threaten the Dauphin's power in southern France. He began the siege of Orleans in 1428. However, the English had dangerously stretched their limited resources. Despite an intensive propaganda campaign in favour of the war, fewer Englishmen wished to serve in France, and Parliament went on believing the military effort should pay for itself. It was these considerations which undoubtedly influenced Bedford to advise against the siege of Orleans.

The appearance of Joan of Arc in the spring of 1429 changed the complexion of the war. In two years she relieved Orleans, inspired the French soldiers to defeat the English at Patay (May 1429) and crowned Charles VII at Rheims (July 1429), before being burnt at Rouen in May 1431. Bedford laboured tirelessly to maintain the deteriorating military position but his authority in France was increasingly being questioned by his younger brother, Humphrey, Duke of Gloucester, and the Council in England. He became progressively more disillusioned, particularly after the death of his wife Anne. The decline in the war effort convinced many on the Council, but notably Cardinal Beaufort, of the need for a peace settlement. The result was the peace conference at Arras in autumn 1435. However, the English delegation refused to discuss Henry VI's claim to the French crown and walked out. This was a disastrous tactic as it left the way open for Philip the Good to withdraw from the English alliance and come to an agreement with Charles VII [**doc. 2**]. With the collapse of the Anglo-Burgundian alliance, the English position in France was no longer viable. To make matters worse Bedford died shortly after the ill-fated conference at Arras.

Bedford's death raised two immediate problems: his replacement and the future conduct of the war. Neither was ever satisfactorily solved; largely because they became issues in the domestic troubles of Henry VI. On the second matter it was decided to introduce a cheap but ultimately disastrous 'scorched-earth' policy, to terrorise the increasingly rebellious English-controlled areas of France into submission. The question of Bedford's successor was a much more important issue. It was in this capacity that Richard, Duke of York, came to the fore for the first time. His father was Richard, Earl of Cambridge, who was executed for treason in 1415. However, it was the death of his uncle, Edward, Duke of York, at Agincourt which set the young Richard on the road to great wealth. The size of his estates was more than doubled when his uncle on his mother's side, Edmund Mortimer, Earl of March, died heirless from the plague in Ireland in 1425. When he came of age in 1432, Richard, Duke of York, was the richest landowner in the kingdom and the holder of the dormant Mortimer claim to the crown (see Genealogies, pp. 100–1, pp. 54–5).

It was probably his leading position in the nobility which marked York out as Bedford's successor. He initially found the position too demanding on account of his inexperience, but in July 1440 he was appointed lieutenant-general for a period of five years. York had to struggle against a continually deteriorating military situation. Paris had fallen in April 1436 and the English were now largely confined to the ever-eroding bastion of Normandy. While in France, York took the opportunity to build up a strong circle of personal supporters, several of whom had served in Bedford's company. They included Sir William Oldhall. As the state of the war grew worse, so did York's relations with the government in London. He can only have resented the dispatch to France of an expedition led by John Beaufort, Duke of Somerset, in August 1443. This undoubtedly helped to sow the seeds of York's deadly rivalry with the Beauforts in the early 1450s. However, relations really broke down over the debts owed to York for his service in France. By the time he returned to England in the autumn of 1445, these amounted to £38,667 (**36**, p. 674). York could not sustain such a loss and probably found himself in serious financial difficulties (see pp. 7–8).

Henry V's son and heir, Prince Henry, had been less than nine months old when he became king in August 1422. Henry VI was to prove a very different personality from his illustrious father. When he came of age in November 1437, he determined on a policy of peace with France. This reached its first stage in 1444 with the 21-month truce signed at Tours. The negotiations also led to the marriage of Henry VI to Margaret of Anjou, the daughter of the French queen's brother, René, Duke of Anjou. Her dowry was arranged at 20,000 francs but she in fact arrived dowerless in England in April 1445. Margaret was only fifteen years old, so her influence over the King in these early years of marriage must not be exaggerated. Nevertheless her presence symbolised the truce and Henry's hopes for peace and she undoubtedly helped sustain his resolve to continue this unpopular policy. The opposition to the truce was led by Humphrey, Duke of Gloucester, who argued that it merely gave the French time to consolidate and prepare for a final assault on the remaining English possessions. His opposition became even more vociferous when rumours began to circulate of Henry's secret cession of Maine on 22 December 1445. Henry made this promise in a personal letter to Charles VII, in an effort to help the negotiations towards a peace settlement [**doc. 3**]. It was the final blow in France. The garrisons were demoralised but it was still difficult to get them to implement the surrender of Maine. It was eventually carried out under threat from a massive French army in March 1448.

It was the truce of Tours and the rumours regarding Maine which probably turned York against Henry's principal adviser, the Earl of Suffolk. York had been on good terms with Suffolk during his last months in France prior to his recall in autumn 1445. Thereafter relations deteriorated and Gloucester's death in 1447 can only have increased his apprehensions (see pp. 16–17). In a clumsy attempt to be rid of York, Henry had him appointed lieutenant of Ireland in July 1447. York refused to go for two years. By treating him as an enemy, Henry and his advisers were turning him into one.

In France, the years after Tours were ones of *malaise* for the English forces. There was confusion in leadership and indiscipline and disorder amongst the troops. Incredibly, it was the English, or more correctly Henry and Suffolk, who restarted the war. In March 1449 François de Surienne attacked and captured the Breton town of Fougères, in the name of the English King. It took just sixteen months and the decisive French victory at Formigny (April 1450) to end the English presence in Normandy in August 1450. The famous war veteran, John Talbot, Earl of Shrewsbury, led a relief force to Gascony which recovered Bordeaux, but in July 1453 he and his men were overwhelmed by the French at Castillon. Talbot was killed and Gascony came into French royal control for the first time, leaving Calais as the sole remnant of the Lancastrian empire.

The loss of France was of the greatest importance in the descent to civil war in England. More than any other factor it discredited the government of Henry VI in the eyes of his subjects. The English failure not only created an atmosphere of national disgrace and outrage at governmental ineptitude, but it also led to a deadly feud that would finally be resolved only by civil war. York blamed the loss of France on his replacement as commander, Edmund Beaufort, Duke of Somerset. To make matters worse, Somerset was allowed first claim on any meagre resources the government made available to repay its debts from service in France. York meanwhile remained heavily out of pocket.

It is wrong to suppose that English knights and soldiers, having been deprived of their French battlegrounds, took to fighting amongst themselves in England. French veterans, from all levels of society, did, it is true, take part in the Wars of the Roses; indeed their experience was much sought after by both sides. However, in general an unprofitable military career in France had long ceased to attract young men. Many seem to have returned 'as the pitiful objects of charity, not the makers of civil war' (**43**, p. 79). Their plight must have had a profound effect on the minds of the people, for here was the stark reality of the government's failure in France. It was no coincidence that it was Kent, the area nearest to France and the armies and fleets of Charles VII, which first lit the torch of rebellion in 1450. The personal effect on Henry VI was bound to be equally shattering. He had striven for a negotiated settlement; now he had encountered humiliating defeat. Castillon was probably the final blow, for within a month the King fell seriously ill.

The nobility*

The internal stability of the medieval state depended upon the relationship between the ruler and his leading subjects, the landed nobility. By the middle of the fifteenth century, the titled nobility in England had largely become a clearly defined, hereditary social grouping. The vast majority of the peerages which they held had

* Asterisked words are explained in the Glossary on page 105.

been bestowed as a consequence of royal summonses to the great Council and Parliament. It was also established convention that the son and heir of a lord summoned to Parliament should inherit his father's title. Therefore the titled nobility had become almost synonymous with England's parliamentary peerage (**48**, Ch. 1; **81**, pp. 86–128).

Titles were only given to men who possessed the landed wealth to support such a dignity. The nobility had to declare their incomes from land in the assessment for the income tax of 1436. These returns must be treated with some caution but they do shed some light on the nature of the fifteenth-century nobility. The lords numbered around fifty, though within this figure the declared incomes varied greatly. Only ten peers admitted to having taxable incomes in excess of £1,000 per annum; and of these, three – the Duke of York, the Earl of Buckingham and the Earl of Warwick – were easily the greatest landowners in the country. These men were preoccupied with land and their position in the social hierarchy, which was determined by their landed wealth. They were fiercely protective of their dynastic interests both at court and in their own localities. Above all, the protection of these interests meant the maintenance of the nobility's right to inherit their estates, offices and influence.

In its relations with these men, the crown had numerous advantages. The monarchy possessed all the traditional and mystical authority of medieval kingship. The king and his leading subjects came from the same social background and indulged in similar pursuits and interests. Therefore it was natural that the crown should respect the nobility as its principal advisers. Yet, as the nobles were preoccupied with their local estates, it was sufficient that the king should only consult them in the great Council on the most important issues of government. Moreover, despite the corporate identity associated with their titles, the nobles were divided amongst themselves. The cause of these divisions was invariably land or its associated phenomenon, position in society. During the later middle ages men seized every opportunity to add acre to acre. The law of real property was in too archaic a condition to meet the demands of so acquisitive a society. There had been no statute of limitations* since the reign of Edward I (1272–1307) and conflicting titles to land existed everywhere. Few families went for more than a few years without being involved in a lawsuit of some kind. The inadequacies of the common law and the growing corruption of the courts merely added to the frustration. Therefore there was a strong impulse to resort to violence to impose a claim. It was vital that the crown did not allow these quarrels to get out of hand. Indeed the settling of noble rivalries was the most important internal task of the royal Council. In fifteenth-century England, the crown relied on the nobles to preserve law and order in their own localities. Therefore if their rivalries were allowed to deteriorate into violence, the implications for the stability of society were disastrous.

Above all, the crown had the power of patronage. The distribution of royal favour stood at the very heart of the relationship between the crown and the nobility in the middle ages. It could take the form of titles, estates, offices, wardships* or marriages, and represented the most rapid form of social advancement. The competition for royal patronage was yet another factor that divided the nobility and should have worked to the advantage of the crown. However, the abuse of royal patronage by individual monarchs carried enormous risks, as the reigns of Edward II and Richard II had shown in the fourteenth century.

It has been argued that rivalries between members of the nobility for lands, patronage and position were turned into a violent struggle for survival by the economic position of the landowning class. The Black Death in 1348–9 caused a steady rise in wage levels for agricultural labourers but a fall in prices. Though the latter picked up, they were hit again by the agricultural and trade decline of the fifteenth century. These economic developments can only have harmed the material wealth of the landowning nobility. Many also suffered from the loss of their lands in France. At the same time noble expenditure was probably rising, due to the increasing number of retainers many lords were maintaining. However, the economic fortunes of the fifteenth-century nobility do not fit into such a neat and simple formula. It is virtually impossible to make any economic generalisations about a country as diverse geographically as England. Some noble families did experience a temporary or permanent decline, usually as a result of the accidents of inheritance (e.g. no male heir) or treason. However, families in these categories, such as the Mowbray Dukes of Norfolk and the Earls of Arundel and Westmorland, were precisely those members of the nobility whose role in the wars was largely inconspicuous. It has been argued that the leading protagonists in the wars were drawing larger incomes from land than their forbears (**48**, pp. 177–186).

However, this theory should not be dismissed out of hand. The awareness of declining landed incomes probably gave a sharper edge to the competition between nobles for royal patronage and lucrative marriages. It also seems likely that Richard, Duke of York, was experiencing a degree of financial difficulty. Research into the Welsh estates of Humphrey, Duke of Buckingham, has revealed a serious decline in landlord profits. This was caused by unpaid rents and judicial dues, the latter always being more important in Wales than England (**51**, pp. 113–4). Buckingham's finances were further strained by the need to provide for his large family. His decision to give active support to the Lancastrians in the autumn of 1459 may well have been partly due to his financial problems and he was certainly amply rewarded after the Rout of Ludford (**81**, pp. 106–7). There seems little doubt that York's Welsh estates suffered similarly. The effect on York's landed income would have been even worse, for his Welsh estates produced more than half the total. Many of these estates appear to have carried a burden of accumulated debt. The arrears for the year 1442 stood at over £3,692, and little more than £1,000 had been recovered by the following year. If at the same time York's expenditure was rising, due to his burgeoning retainer wage bill, then 'poverty may, after all, have been the spur to political gangsterism' (**83**, p. 302). In these circumstances the failure of the crown to pay the huge sums York was owed from the war assumes a striking importance, particularly when his rival Somerset was repaid for his services in spite of his record in France. Whenever he succeeded in imposing himself on the government, York invariably voted himself sums of money for his services. Under the Act of Accord York granted himself and his sons 10,000 marks per annum from the royal revenues to support their new position as heirs to Henry VI [**doc. 14**]. Such was his concern for the state of the royal finances! There is also evidence of York trying to mortgage or sell two of his manors in Wales, a development almost unheard of amongst the land-hungry nobility of fifteenth-century England (**83**).

The rivalry between York and Somerset was only one of many which characterise the middle years of the fifteenth century. They burst into violence in various parts of the country, the most infamous being that between the Nevilles and the Percies in the north. Law and order in these areas collapsed. There is a great deal of truth in the oft-quoted comment that the Wars of the Roses were 'the outcome of an escalation of private feuds' (**58**, p. 27). However, the feuds alone were not the cause of the wars; they were a manifestation of the basic reason – the weak faction-ridden rule of Henry VI. Royal favour and patronage exacerbated rather than assuaged the rivalries of the nobility.

The overriding characteristic of the English nobility when

confronted by the misrule of Henry VI was caution. They sympathised with York's attempts to reform the government, but they would not follow him into armed rebellion and were dismayed when he finally claimed the throne in 1460. They were the social and economic establishment and as such had more to lose than most. They would not lightly hazard their estates and position in society by resorting to rebellion. The high-point of noble participation in the wars was during the period 1459–61. It has been calculated that there were sixty secular lords in September 1459, a further ten were created or came of age between then and March 1461, and fifty-six out of the seventy participated in the fighting of 1459–61 (**35**, p. 200). Only a small minority had the strongest of feelings either way. Lord Rivers spoke for many in 1461 when he pledged his loyalty to Edward IV on the grounds that the cause of Henry VI was 'irretrievably' lost (**76**, p. 103). Yet one must not exaggerate the influence of the 'trimmers'. Enough nobles were prepared to support Edward IV in 1461 to overthrow the House of Lancaster. The turning-point in Yorkist support was the Parliament of Devils in November 1459 when the Lancastrians disinherited the exiled Yorkist earls and their families. Henry VI's government had challenged the right of inheritance. The Duke of York made a similar misjudgement in the following year. When he disinherited Prince Edward, he earned the wrath of Margaret of Anjou and many nobles who rallied to the Lancastrian cause. The result was the battle of Wakefield and the nadir of Yorkist fortunes.

Livery and maintenance

Livery and maintenance, or – as it is more commonly but erroneously called – 'bastard feudalism', was the network of social, economic and political relationships that gave cohesion to English society in the later middle ages. It derived from the old military feudalism of Anglo-Norman England. At the heart of both was the feudal concept of vassalic commendation, the relationship between a lord and his vassal or retainer. However, the rigid military relationship of Norman times had been changed out of all recognition by the growing complexity of medieval society. Land and wealth were no longer the sole prerogative of a military élite. Later medieval families rose through trade, service in administration and the professions, notably the law. This social mobility reflected the growth in the economy, the scope of medieval government and the legal system. It was these and other developments in English society which determined the nature of the relationships between a lord and his retainers in the later middle ages.

Whereas the nature of these relationships was varied, the basic concern of those involved was the same: land. Landed wealth was the creation and reflection of a family's political, social and economic standing. The need of landowners to protect, maintain and expand their estates generated a great variety of services – administrative, legal, religious, technical as well as military – in the later middle ages. The mode of maintaining men in these services was invariably the indenture, a form of contract. Only a small number of these indentures have survived but they generally have one overriding characteristic: the period of service is life [**doc. 15**]. In return the lord would retain his men through cash fees and life annuities. These were not, of course, the only means of retaining. A lord had a wide range of offices in his gift, and could offer appointments as stewards, receivers, constables of castles, keepers of forests and so on (**81**, pp. 102–3). This network of lord and man extended far beyond the confines of the lord's household. The stability of a lord's estate depended upon a peaceful co-existence with the neighbouring landowners. The latter might well be retained by indenture but could also be tenants of the lord, or just friends and 'well-willers'. These men were more a part of the lord's affinity than his retinue.

Livery and maintenance is most usually associated with the great noble families. The patronage of such lords was eagerly sought after, while they themselves were anxious to recruit clientage. They attracted not only lesser men but also the local gentry.* This enabled the nobles to raise a military force quickly, to exercise local influence, and as a corollary of these, to attain an importance in national politics. In return for support, the nobles could not only dispense fees, grants and offices, but they could often – as the Duke of Suffolk did to great advantage in the 1440s – use their standing at court to influence the direction of royal patronage. Such rewards supplemented the financial sums stipulated in the indentures, which outside the Marcher areas were generally not very substantial. However, these elements were peripheral to the main concern of the smaller landowners or gentry, once again that of land. Like the nobility, they were preoccupied with the protection, extension and transmission by inheritance of their estates.

The relationship between a lord and his man also came to dominate local government and justice. In this way livery and maintenance reversed important administrative developments which dated back to the twelfth century. Henry II and his successors had increased crown authority by expanding the jurisdiction of the common law and the royal courts. This led to a new relationship between the crown and the gentry. The latter were increasingly called upon to act as royal officials in the courts and local government, eventually being summoned as shire knights to Parliament. In the course of the fourteenth century the nobility wrested control of local government from the royal bureaucracy and exploited it in their own interests. The key local officials were the JPs and above all, the sheriffs. The latter were responsible for bringing defendants to court, assembling juries and carrying out verdicts. By influencing JPs and sheriffs, the lord could settle satisfactorily the pleas of his own retainers and throw out those of his opponents. In the fifteenth century the office of sheriff was notorious for corruption and bribery. When the law proved ineffective, the lord could resort to force. This was seen as a legitimate appeal to divine judgement. Therefore by dominating local administration, either by influence or force, the lord looked after the interests of his retainers and friends, and demonstrated his ability to provide 'good lordship'. In this way he attracted yet more support. This was crucial for the lord, as the size of his affinity determined his position in the nobility and his influence in national politics.

In some areas – notably the north, East Anglia and the south-west – where noble families struggled for regional supremacy, rival groups of gentry inevitably attached themselves to rival lords. However, it is now clear that the commercial exploitation of the retaining system by the Paston family from East Anglia, so graphically described in their letters, was not typical of the gentry as a whole. Once again it is very difficult to generalise. Another East Anglian gentleman, John Hopton, lived outside any social grouping of lord/retainer. He was wealthy and enterprising but uninterested in local or national politics (**53**). Between the Pastons at one extreme and Hopton at the other lay the vast majority of the gentry. Nor was the loyalty of the gentry given to a lord unquestioningly; they could prove as pragmatic in protecting their interests as the nobles. In March 1471, the Earl of Warwick took the trouble of penning his own postscript to a letter to Sir Henry Vernon, imploring him to come with as many troops as possible. He wrote: 'Henry I pray you ffayle not now as ever I may do ffor yow' (**76**, p. 111). Vernon was unmoved and did not fight at Barnet where Warwick was killed.

These social ties and relationships were essential in later medieval society. In the absence of a police force or a standing army the personal bond between a lord and a man was the basis of peace in the countryside. The crown relied on the nobility to maintain local law and order and thus gave them a high degree of independence in their areas. An effective monarch like Henry V could control livery and maintenance by controlling the nobles. The decline began during the minority of Henry VI when the nobles of the Council inevitably adopted a policy of non-interference in each others' local affairs. Henry VI did nothing to reverse this trend after he came of age in 1437. Indeed his partisan policies exacerbated the rivalries in the shires. The abuses of livery and maintenance developed without restraint in these years.

Part Two: Analysis: Lancastrians and Yorkists 1437–1485

2 The Reign of Henry VI 1437–1450

Amid great rejoicing, Henry of Windsor, the only child of Henry V and Queen Catherine, was born on 6 December 1421. His reign was destined to be one of the most disastrous in English history. It began with a fifteen-year minority and ended in the King's deposition and civil war. Henry became King of England while less than nine months old, on 31 August 1422. Within two months he was the first and last King of the dual monarchy of England and France, following the death of his French grandfather, Charles VI, in October 1422.

In medieval government so much was dependent upon the character of the king, that it might be expected that the accession of an infant to the English throne would lead to political and military collapse. The recent experience of Richard II's minority certainly pointed in that direction, but on this occasion it proved otherwise. Henry VI was much younger than Richard II had been and the governing Council was able to achieve a much greater coherence and efficiency. There was an inevitable decline after the death of Henry V, but the minority Council strove, not without success, to continue his policies. Neither the internal state of England or the war in France were hopeless causes when Henry VI came of age in 1437. This is not to deny that the nobles on the Council used their new-found power to advance their own family interests. However, it is a testimony to their collective abilities that they did not allow their inevitable rivalries to plunge the country into anarchy and chaos.

The greatest and most dangerous of these rivalries was between Humphrey, Duke of Gloucester, and Henry Beaufort, Cardinal and Bishop of Winchester. Gloucester resented the way in which Henry V's will, naming him as Henry VI's principal guardian and protector, had been set aside by the rest of the nobility. His resentment came to focus on Henry Beaufort, who presumably was the most powerful advocate of conciliar rule. Gloucester was very popular in the country, in stark contrast to his standing amongst the nobility. He had served with distinction in France and been wounded at Agincourt. A clever and cultured man, Gloucester was also intensely ambitious, self-seeking and on occasions irresponsible. His ambitions in Hainault cut right across the crucial Anglo-Burgundian alliance.

Henry Beaufort was the second son of John of Gaunt's bastard line from Catherine Swynford (see Genealogies, p. 102). The family was legitimised in 1397, the year in which Beaufort embarked upon his illustrious career in the Church and politics. In 1404 he was consecrated Bishop of Winchester, which brought him the richest diocese in England with estates worth possibly £4,000 per annum. Beaufort utilised this wealth to make a series of large loans to the crown. Between his first loan in 1404 and the last in 1446, he lent and was repaid £212,330, which represented about one third of the total loans to the crown in the period. Gloucester can only have felt a profound jealousy at this wealth. In comparison he was poorly endowed with lands and was often short of money. Gloucester accused Beaufort of usury, forbidden under Church law, but he could never prove the charge and there is no evidence that the Cardinal was imposing any terms of interest. Beaufort's motives for the loans were not financial; above all, he was a politician and a dynast. His wealth and the crown's indebtedness to him enabled him to challenge the leadership in Council claimed by Gloucester and to build up his own group of supporters. In his final years, Beaufort sought to establish his nephews in the forefront of the English nobility. This engendered a reaction which eventually engulfed not only the Beauforts but also the Lancastrian dynasty.

Henry VI began to involve himself in affairs of state from the middle of the 1430s. In November 1437, while still less than sixteen years old, he declared himself to have come of age, and government reverted to the appearance of normality under an 'adult' king. The Council returned to its traditional advisory role. The interests of the young King were largely confined to the distribution of royal patronage and his desire for peace in France. While the country yearned for another warrior king in the mould of Henry V, Henry showed himself to be wholly uninterested in military matters. He was the first post-1066 king not to lead an English army against a foreign enemy. Henry was concerned with peace and seemingly at any price.

Henry's desire for peace made him naturally gravitate towards Cardinal Beaufort and away from his uncle Gloucester, who had succeeded Bedford as the great advocate of the war. By 1439 Gloucester had lost all influence over the King, who was surrounded and dominated by the Cardinal and his family. The Beauforts benefited greatly from the unprecedented dispersal of patronage inspired by Henry VI in the years after 1437. For example, eleven associates of the family were promoted to the office of sheriff in the years 1437–41, giving them great influence in the shires concerned (**36**, p. 336). However, the most influential adviser was William de la Pole, Earl of Suffolk, particularly after the semi-retirement and death in 1447 of Cardinal Beaufort. Suffolk's rise was based on his personal relationship with the King. He established a domination over the household after being appointed steward in 1433 and grasped every opportunity to augment his rather modest landed inheritance. Henry showered him with crown estates and offices. He made him a marquis in 1444, Chamberlain in 1447 and finally, in 1448 a duke – a title normally reserved for members of the royal family.

This dispersal of titles, lands and offices was repeated at every level of government. Within a decade of 1437 royal patronage had built up a labyrinth of household officials and royal servants throughout the shires of England and Wales. The greatest concentration was to be found in the south, East Anglia and the south-east, the areas closest to London and the court. Suffolk in particular was active in advancing his dependants to positions of influence in this important area. With some justification these years have been called the 'golden age of the household official' (**36**, p. 334). The influence of the household extended to the episcopate. Suffolk was undoubtedly the influence behind the appointment of Adam Moleyns to the see of Chichester in September 1445. Several other prominent household officials were also rewarded with bishoprics. One of Suffolk's associates, John Kemp, became Archbishop of Canterbury in July 1453. There was nothing unusual in constructing an affinity in this manner in the later middle ages. Other families like the Nevilles, Percies, Beauchamps and Staffords were also spreading their influence in society below them, if on a smaller scale. It was in fact the size and expense of Henry's household affinity and their monopoly and abuse of crown patronage which aroused the resentment of the other nobles.

At both a central and a local level, Henry's rule became associated with political faction. Concern at this state of affairs was expressed very early in the reign. The Council urged Henry to change his habits, while the Commons in Parliament correctly focused on the malign role of the household and complained that royal favour was destroying the impartiality of royal justice. There is no evidence that these repeated complaints had any effect on Henry. The King's lavish distribution of royal patronage also greatly exacerbated the parlous financial position of the crown. The war remained a continual burden on the royal finances as Parliament only intermittently granted taxation, usually in crisis years like 1436. To make matters worse, Henry was not only generous to members of his household. He lavished money on his foundations at Eton and King's College, Cambridge. By 1450 the Lancastrian government was to all intents and purposes bankrupt. The burden of accumulated debt had spiralled to £372,000 (**36**, p. 377). The death of Cardinal Beaufort in April 1447 removed the government's chief creditor, though his executors did make a posthumous loan of nearly £10,000 in 1449. The Italian bankers and merchants, who had also financed the royal government, were very reluctant to risk any further money and lent only £1,000 to the crown in the last decade of Henry VI's reign (**54**, p. 378). This limited the government's freedom of action and may well have partly influenced Henry in his most disastrous policy decision: peace at any price in France.

There seems little doubt that Henry was the inspiration behind the peace policy. Many historians have pointed an accusing finger at Suffolk, as did most contemporaries. However, he seems to have used his considerable influence almost exclusively for his own financial advantage. He appears to have been very reluctant to undertake the Tours peace mission in 1444, probably realising that he would receive the blame for this unpopular initiative. In foreign policy Suffolk was the 'faithful executant' rather than the inspiration (**61**, pp. 223–4). This is not to remove all responsibility from him. As the King's principal adviser, he should have influenced constructively a man who was patently weak and incapable of ruling. There is no evidence that Suffolk ever did so.

Henry VI reacted sharply to criticism of his policy. His vindictiveness became focused on his own heir, the Duke of Gloucester. The King and Suffolk were behind the scandal which destroyed Gloucester's second wife Eleanor Cobham in 1441. She was arrested and charged with sorcery, found guilty and exiled after performing public penance. Gloucester himself was not implicated, but he was seriously discredited and his marriage was annulled. As the war went from bad to worse, many of the nobles, even Gloucester, began to favour a peace settlement, but one negotiated from a position of strength. Henry's policy of peace through concessions, illustrated by the secret surrender of Maine, was hardly what they had in mind. Gloucester violently opposed the royal policy and his popular esteem rose dramatically from the depths of 1441. His opposition became so outspoken and the rumours regarding the cession of Maine so damaging that the King determined to silence him. At the same time Henry, no doubt influenced by Suffolk and Margaret of Anjou, seems to have believed that Gloucester was plotting to take the throne by violence.

In February 1447, Parliament was summoned to Bury St Edmunds, a centre of Suffolk influence, so that it would condemn Gloucester for treason. When Gloucester arrived on 18 February he was promptly arrested. Five days later he was dead, probably from natural causes, though the shock of arrest cannot have helped. There were widespread rumours of murder, as he had died in the hands of his enemies. Gloucester's death left Richard, Duke of York, as heir presumptive.

3 Cade's Rebellion and the Emergence of York 1450–1453

By the end of the 1440s there was widespread dissatisfaction at Lancastrian rule. The reasons were simple – the state of the war in France and the breakdown in law and order. Many contemporaries must have done the same as one pro-Yorkist writer and pondered the striking contrasts betwen the rule of Henry VI and that of his father [**doc. 6**]. The crisis that ensued in 1450 questioned the nature of Henry VI's faction-dominated government.

In the face of the deteriorating position in Normandy, Parliament met in February 1449. The Commons only granted a minimal half-tenth and fifteenth in taxation. They attacked the household and demanded an act of Resumption* as the price of any further grant of taxation. Parliament was dissolved but the growing disaster in France led to its recall in November 1449. Violent resistance soon followed in the country. In January 1450 Adam Moleyns was lynched by unpaid soldiers at Portsmouth. Before his death he was alleged to have made serious charges against Suffolk regarding the surrender of Maine. When Parliament reconvened later in the month, the Commons proceeded to impeach Suffolk for treason. He was principally charged with mismanaging foreign policy and with 'insatiable covetise' which had led him to exploit his position as the leading royal adviser for financial profit, thereby impoverishing the crown. The charges were never properly examined as Henry intervened and exiled Suffolk for five years. However, Suffolk's ship was intercepted in the Channel and he was beheaded on behalf of the 'community of the realm', by the crew of the *Nicholas of the Tower* [**doc. 7**].

The self-confidence of the household and government was badly shaken by the impeachment of Suffolk. It was decided to placate the Commons by accepting an act of Resumption 'in summe but nat in alle' in May 1450. This was a partial defeat for Henry's government but by the end of May an even greater threat had appeared from the social class who usually played little part in matters of state – the peasants. Large numbers of Kentish peasants assembled in the Ashford area and marched to Blackheath. The rising spread to Essex and contingents came from there. In these early stages the peasants were well-ordered, showing a firm leadership and a strong common purpose. The identity of the rebel leader remains something of a mystery. Contemporaries were unanimous in calling him John Cade and the official order for his arrest says he was born in Ireland, served in the household of a Sussex knight and fled to France after murdering a pregnant woman [**doc. 8**]. However, these revelations probably reflect the government's determination to blacken his reputation. It seems likely that he came from the lower ranks of society, though Cade himself claimed that his name was John Mortimer and for a time many believed that he was related to the Duke of York. The government claimed that the rebels wished to put York on the throne, but there is no impartial evidence to support this. Neither York nor his chamberlain, Sir William Oldhall, seem to have instigated the rebellion, as the later Tudor historians and Shakespeare believed. York's conduct in 1450 was more that of a man reacting to events than initiating them. He did not return to England until two months after the revolt had ended. The rebels only demanded that York and other members of the wider royal family, such as the Dukes of Buckingham and Exeter, should be given their rightful position on the royal Council. There was no mention of the crown.

A striking characteristic of the rebellion was the production of well-publicised manifestoes, incorporating a skilful mixture of national and local grievances. It is clear that the Kentishmen regarded themselves as petitioners backing up the demands of Parliament, rather than rebels. Political reform was their desire, not revolution. They affirmed their loyalty to Henry VI and attacked his 'evil' advisers for monopolising royal patronage and ruling oppressively. The specifically Kentish grievances were a microcosm of the general political *malaise*. They were dominated by the activities of the household officials in the area, principally Lord Saye, Treasurer of England, and his son-in-law William Crowemer. It is perfectly in character that the King should have visited Kent nine times between 1438 and 1448 and shown no concern for the activities of these men (**61**, p. 125). The rebel demands centred on the replacement of the household officials as the King's advisers by lords of the 'trew blode of [the] realme', principally York. They also called for an inquiry into whether the growing disaster in France was the result of treason.

Henry VI wavered between intransigence and conciliation before he left London on 25 June for Kenilworth. The loyalty of his own troops had been put in doubt when clashes with the rebels occurred near Sevenoaks. His weak *volte-face* of imprisoning Saye and Crowemer impressed no-one and Henry took flight, abandoning his capital to the rebels. They entered the city, but despite Cade's good intentions the peasant army soon degenerated into a looting and burning mob. Saye and Crowemer were taken from the Tower and executed. The unrest was now beginning to spread. In Wiltshire, another household official, William Aiscough, Bishop of Salisbury, was dragged from a church and beheaded. Mobs also threatened the Bishops of Lichfield and Norwich. The behaviour of the rebels in London soon turned the citizens against them. On the night of 5 July the Londoners cleared them from the streets and gained control of the city end of London Bridge, preventing any further rebel access from Southwark. The remnants of the government in the area seized their chance and at the instance of Margaret of Anjou, who was at Greenwich, offered a free pardon to the rebels if they dispersed. Cade accepted and the rebels left London. Most went home, though Cade himself later broke the pardon and was killed while resisting arrest.

The government still did not feel strong enough to suppress the last vestiges of the rebellion and dispatched a series of judicial commissions to inquire into local grievances in Kent. Nevertheless it had rather shakily survived both the fall of Suffolk and the rebellion. Many of the personnel in the government had not lived through the year, but the nature of Henry's rule remained unchanged. There was to be no respite from his weak, faction-ridden government for another three years, and then it was to prove only temporary.

An even more dangerous challenge to the government presented itself later in the year. Early in September 1450 York returned unannounced from Ireland. His return was probably inspired by genuine personal grievances. He wished to clear his name, which had been linked with treasonable movements, and thus protect his position as heir presumptive. York can also only have felt resentment at the treatment of Somerset, his replacement as commander in France. Somerset had presided over the loss of France and yet on his return to England had rejoined the Council and been made Constable of England. It is unlikely that York's financial position had greatly improved. Therefore his resentment was exacerbated by Somerset receiving first claim on any available royal funds for repayment of war debts. Finally York may well have feared that Henry might recognise Somerset as his heir (see p. 55).

York prepared two bills of complaint which the King received in late September 1450. The first was concerned with the personal grievances outlined above – his fear of attainder, his position as heir, his debts and the fact that his counsel had been ignored. The opportunism of York and his advisers is demonstrated by the second bill. Having gauged the mood in the country he combined his own grievances with those expressed in Parliament and Cade's Rebellion. York had thus taken the first step towards appealing for support by converting personal grievances into a general bid for public sympathy. Yet York possessed serious defects as a political leader. He was a proud, reserved and essentially aloof figure. Policies conceived largely in self-interest were unlikely to win committed noble support and this accounts for his failure in the years 1450–3.

York presented himself as the champion of justice and the destroyer of corruption. He enlisted the support of the Commons in the Parliament which opened in November. The Parliament was another difficult one but the government survived it. England remained essentially a personal monarchy and it was difficult for any subject, however great, to control the government against the King's will. The government reacted by placating the Commons with a more effective act of Resumption and the promise of a renewed effort to re-establish law and order in the shires. The Commons hoped the government had learnt the error of its ways and gave no trouble when Parliament was dissolved in June 1451.

York found himself isolated and distrusted. Meanwhile Henry had shown his confidence in Somerset by making him Captain of Calais, thereby giving him control of the largest military garrison at the crown's disposal. Henry clearly had no intention of reforming his household. York was therefore left with no real alternative but to try to impose himself by force, particularly as his position as heir presumptive now seemed in jeopardy. In the final parliamentary session, Thomas Yonge, one of York's councillors and MP for Bristol, had proposed that York should be formally declared heir apparent [**doc. 9**]. He found himself in the Tower for his pains.

Just as Yonge's plea misfired so did York's rebellion in February 1452. York marched with his supporters from the Welsh Marches, but despite his intensive propaganda campaign the men of Kent stayed at home. Nor were any nobles, other than the riotous Earl of Devon and his associate Lord Cobham, prepared to join him. The royal forces were far larger, but significant elements within them – notably Humphrey, Duke of Buckingham, and the Neville Earls of Salisbury and Warwick – urged moderation on the King. York was prevailed upon to face military facts and he submitted to Henry at Blackheath on 2 March. At the meeting York presented articles of complaint against Somerset, but the King was unmoved. York was forced to take a solemn oath of allegiance to Henry in St Paul's Cathedral.

Despite resorting to force, York had failed to impose himself and his policies on the King. He now found himself completely isolated. Talbot's short-lived success in Gascony and Henry's judicial progresses through southern England turned the Parliament of March 1453 completely against York. The Commons voted the King generous taxation and attainted York's chamberlain, Sir William Oldhall, for treason, though no mention was made of the Duke himself. However, just as suddenly, York's fortunes changed dramatically for the better.

4 The Fall of the House of Lancaster 1453–1461

In early August 1453, Henry VI lapsed into a mental stupor at the royal hunting lodge at Clarendon, near Salisbury. For eighteen months the King was deprived of all senses and physical movement. His illness raised two important issues: the question of the succession and the nature of future government.

The birth of Henry's son, Prince Edward, on 13 October 1453 seemed to settle the vexed question of the succession but made the issue of government more pressing than ever. The country now faced the prospect of an incapacitated King, or, if Henry should die, another long minority. In the ensuing arguments over the government, Margaret of Anjou emerged as 'the champion of Lancastrian interests' (**61**, p. 277). A strong-willed woman, Margaret had given Henry invaluable support in the pursuit of his peace policy, and had shown much courage and a capacity for decision-making in the crisis of Cade's Rebellion. However, it was only now, her maternal instincts aroused by the birth of her son, that she really came to the front of the political stage. She was determined to protect his inheritance by whatever means necessary.

The government played for time, refusing at first to admit that Henry was ill. Shortly before Christmas, Somerset was imprisoned in the Tower, both as a conciliatory move and for his own protection. However, it soon became apparent that Henry was not going to recover quickly. By early January 1454 Margaret had formulated plans to become regent. Such a concept appalled the nobility, who were gradually coming over to the side of York. Easily the most important noble family to gravitate towards York was the Nevilles. The furtherance of their feud with the Percies in the north made it likely that they would come to associate with either the government or York. By late 1453 the Earl of Salisbury was moving in the direction of the latter, but the die was really cast by the ambitions of his eldest son, the Earl of Warwick.

In July 1449 Richard Neville had been created Earl of Warwick in right of his wife, Anne Beauchamp. It was yet another example of the rise of the Neville family through advantageous marriages.

This gave the new Earl vast estates in the midlands, the south and southern Wales. It was in the latter that he fell foul of Henry VI's partisan use of government. In early 1453 Henry granted the Duke of Somerset the keeping of the great Marcher lordship of Glamorgan. However, Warwick had held the lordship since 1450 and he therefore prepared to resist the royal will by force. He began to be associated with Somerset's greatest enemy, the Duke of York, and was followed by the rest of the Neville family.

While the Nevilles became stalwart supporters of York, other members of the nobility, though sympathetic to York's claim to be protector, adopted a more cautious approach. In February 1454 Parliament assembled, but attendance was so poor that for the only known time in English medieval history, fines were imposed on peers for non-attendance (**82**). However, this was only a temporary setback for York who needed active noble support to become protector. The death of John Kemp, Archbishop of Canterbury, in March meant that royal authority had to be exercised in the appointment of his successor. Therefore the nature of future government had to be resolved. A delegation of lords visited the King but found him incapable of any communication, let alone a decision on Kemp's successor. Therefore, on 27 March York was made Protector [**doc 10**].

York's rule reflects some credit on him. He made a number of partisan moves – for instance, appointing the Earl of Salisbury chancellor – but his Council included all shades of political opinion, reflecting York's lack of committed noble support. York was unable to bring Somerset to trial, but he did replace him as Captain of Calais. He also introduced stringent reductions in the size and expenditure of the royal household and was able to restore some semblance of law and order in the north. Unfortunately in a dynastic sense the protectorate exacerbated the divisions between York and the Lancastrian faction. York may well have interpreted his appointment as Protector as a sign of baronial favour towards his dynastic position and the prelude to a future claim for the crown. Margaret of Anjou certainly saw it as such. She greatly resented York's nomination as Protector and clearly saw him as a direct threat to her son.

Henry VI recovered at Christmas 1454 [**doc. 11**] – an event which one historian has called 'a national disaster' (**58**, p. 159) – and early in 1455 York's protectorate came to an end. There was an immediate reaction against him and his allies. Somerset was released from prison and restored to the captaincy of Calais. The

Earl of Salisbury was either dismissed or resigned as chancellor. York and the Nevilles fled north, where they resolved to impose their will on the King by force if necessary. Margaret and Somerset probably convinced Henry that they were plotting treason and he summoned them to appear before a carefully chosen great Council at Leicester, in the heart of Lancastrian territory, on 21 May. The parallels with Gloucester's fate in 1447 were not lost on York and the Nevilles. They came in force and took the Lancastrians by surprise. Somerset hurriedly raised a force but the Yorkists had a superiority in both numbers and, according to several accounts, fighting qualities.

Negotiations quickly foundered and the fighting started. The battle of St Albans (22 May 1455) was little more than a skirmish, with possibly only sixty men being killed, but they included Somerset and Henry Percy, Earl of Northumberland. The King himself was wounded by an arrow. However, St Albans represented only a short-term success for York. He had removed Somerset but he was still confronted by a weak, suspicious King, under the influence of his avowed enemies, Margaret and the household. York still commanded little committed noble support apart from the Nevilles. This dictated a policy of reconciliation. When Parliament assembled in July the Yorkists therefore reaffirmed their allegiance to the King. All blame for the violence at St Albans was directed at Somerset and his associates.

There has been much discussion about Henry's state of health in the months after St Albans but it does seem likely that he suffered some sort of relapse in the autumn of 1455. This can be the only plausible reason for York's second protectorate in November. It lasted until February 1456, by which time Henry had made something of a recovery. In many respects the most important Yorkist gain from these months was Warwick's appointment as Captain of Calais. The town subsequently became a Yorkist base and in effect 'the seat of an alternative government' (**72**, p. 52).

The remarkable aspect of the years 1456–9 is that civil war did not break out again before 1459. Henry was now 'a pathetic shadow of a king' (**36**, p. 775). He made several attempts at reconciliation with the Yorkists, but his health was failing again. In any case the divisions were too deep, and events like the famous 'Loveday' of 24 March 1458, when the rival parties marched arm-in-arm to St Paul's Cathedral, were wholly superficial and impractical. In these years, at the insistence of Margaret, the government increasingly withdrew to the Lancastrian strongholds in the midlands. Normal political life collapsed and law and order again deteriorated in the shires. Margaret also began building up her own forces, notably in north Wales and Cheshire [**doc. 12**].

By 1459 Margaret, encouraged by her new ally, the Duke of Buckingham, and the sons of the 'victims' of St Albans, had finally convinced Henry VI that York was plotting to take the throne. It was therefore decided at an exclusively Lancastrian great Council meeting held at Coventry in June 1459, to destroy the Yorkists by force. The Yorkist leaders were indicted for treason. They responded by raising their forces in another attempt to gain a hearing from the King, but this was merely seen as a sign of treason. York remained in the Welsh Marches, where it was planned that the Nevilles would join him. The Lancastrians were determined to prevent this Yorkist concentration. Salisbury, coming from Yorkshire, was intercepted by Margaret's Cheshiremen under Lord Audley at Blore Heath in Shropshire on 23 September. Salisbury fought his way through, inflicting heavy losses on the Cheshiremen, and Audley was himself killed.

York, Salisbury and Warwick prepared to make their stand at Ludford Bridge, near Ludlow. They issued an appeal to the King, cataloguing the ills of the kingdom which they attributed to his evil advisers. However, Henry appears to have been stiffened against the Yorkists by events at Blore Heath. He offered a pardon to them (excluding Salisbury) provided they surrendered within six days. The Yorkists ignored this offer but their position was being undermined. They spread a rumour that Henry was dead, to counter the stigma of opposing the King in arms which was eroding their forces. It proved to no avail. When the Calais men under Andrew Trollope deserted to the Lancastrians, the Yorkists decided on flight. In the 'Rout of Ludford' on 12–13 October 1459, York and his second son, the Earl of Rutland, fled to Ireland; Salisbury, Warwick and York's eldest son, the Earl of March, to Devon, from where they took ship to Calais.

The Lancastrians consolidated their bloodless victory at the notorious 'Parliament of Devils' held at Coventry in November 1459. The Yorkist leaders were attainted for treason and sentenced to death. Their lands were forfeited but the Lancastrians went even further, barring all their heirs from succeeding to the entailed estates [**doc. 13**]. This was in gross violation of the convention that entailed land was sacrosanct, even for treason. For this reason, despite the oath of allegiance to Henry taken by the nobility at Coventry, a significant part of the baronage began to move towards York.

The Yorkists made a remarkable recovery from the 'Rout of Ludford'. In this the position of Calais proved crucial. Warwick raised money by piracy, which made him a national hero, and an intensive propaganda campaign was launched against the government. In June 1460 Salisbury, Warwick and March landed at Sandwich in yet another attempt to rescue Henry VI from the control of evil advisers. Kent rallied to their support and on 2 July they were admitted to London, where the trade recession and the favour shown to foreign merchants had turned the mercantile interests against the government. The Yorkists left the city quickly to confront the King at Northampton. Only Salisbury was left behind to deal with the royalist garrison in the Tower. As in 1455 and 1459, the Yorkists sought a hearing from the King, but, as on those occasions, negotiations proved fruitless. The battle of Northampton on 10 July was decided by the treachery of Lord Grey of Ruthin in favour of the Yorkists. Henry was captured and Buckingham killed, but Margaret and Prince Edward escaped to the north.

The only curious feature of the Yorkist success was the behaviour of the Duke of York. He did not return to England until 8 September, just in time for the assembly of Parliament early in October. Significantly he was already adopting outward signs of monarchy. When York arrived at Westminster Hall on 10 October, he strode through the assembled lords and laid his hand on the empty throne. His action was as unexpected as it was unwelcome. No-one was more surprised than the Nevilles, but York was not going to be denied. Six days later he formally asserted his claim to the crown. However, the judges were not prepared to give a verdict and the nobles refused to renege on their oaths of loyalty to Henry VI. Neither would they take a firm stand against York. The result was the Act of Accord, which, in the style of the treaty of Troyes, recognised Henry as King for the rest of his life but disinherited Prince Edward and gave the succession to York and his heirs [**doc. 14**].

York can only have been disappointed at the Act of Accord, as he was ten years older than the King. However, he had more pressing problems with the large Lancastrian army in the north. Though some of the nobility had rallied to the Yorkists, the majority still adhered to the King. York responded by setting off for the north with Salisbury and Rutland in early December 1460. It was there that he made his final miscalculation, for as he was leaving Sandal Castle he was attacked by a much larger Lancastrian army and defeated at the battle of Wakefield on 30 December. York and

Rutland were killed and Salisbury was captured and executed. The severed heads of York and Salisbury were impaled on Micklegate Bar at York, the former adorned with a paper crown.

The victorious Lancastrian army came south in an orgy of looting and murder. This served to stiffen resistance in the south. Warwick determined to intercept the Lancastrians at St Albans but his scouts failed him and he was taken partially by surprise. He might still have carried the day but treachery intervened to give the Lancastrians victory in the second battle of St Albans on 17 February 1461. Margaret was reunited with Henry, whom Warwick had taken to the battle. The Lancastrians continued their march south and Margaret opened negotiations with the Londoners. The latter were concerned about the behaviour of her northern troops and, as a conciliatory move, Margaret withdrew the main part of her forces to Dunstable. This gave time for a new Yorkist saviour to come to the rescue of the capital.

In December 1460 the Earl of March had gone to Wales, where he had defeated the Lancastrians under Jasper Tudor at the battle of Mortimer's Cross (2 or 3 February 1461). He then joined the defeated Warwick in the Cotswolds and they marched back to London. Margaret, probably trusting to her instinct of always retreating to the Lancastrian north in a crisis, and with her army short of food, withdrew to the north. This gave the Yorkists valuable breathing space. Nevertheless they were in a weak position, being unable to command any real obedience from the people. To strengthen their position March decided to take the throne and on 4 March 1461 he was proclaimed king as Edward IV. He then raised an army and headed north to confront the formidable Lancastrian forces. In the midlands he was joined by Warwick. After a preliminary skirmish with the Lancastrians at Ferrybridge the two armies clashed in a raging snow storm at Towton on Palm Sunday, 29 March. In a long and bloody struggle the Yorkists emerged triumphant.

5 The First Reign of Edward IV 1461–1469

The Yorkist victory at Towton established Edward IV on the throne. Edward was to prove an infinitely more able monarch than Henry VI but his position remained precarious for the next decade [**doc. 16**]. He faced determined opposition from diehard Lancastrians and, later, disaffected Yorkists. Indeed Edward's real achievement lay in gaining and then, albeit with difficulties, keeping power. In this his military ability proved decisive.

Henry VI, Margaret of Anjou and Prince Edward had not been present at Towton. They fled to Scotland where they were joined by the survivors from the battle, including the Dukes of Somerset and Exeter. Towton also weakened the power of the staunch Lancastrian families in the north, notably the Percies, but it was still in their region that the greatest opposition to Yorkist rule came. Yet the Lancastrians were unable to mount an effective domestic rebellion. This was partly due to the losses suffered at Towton but perhaps more to Lancastrian strategy. Margaret of Anjou and her advisers rejected the Yorkist device of stimulating domestic insurrection by exploiting popular discontent. Instead they relied upon foreign support and effectively 'internationalised' the struggle (**35**, pp. 55–6).

Edward's survival in the first years of his reign depended upon crushing the Lancastrian insurrections in the north and also Wales and neutralising Margaret's foreign support. In the former he was indebted to the Neville family. The Earl of Warwick was appointed warden of both the eastern and western Marches in July 1461, where he was more than ably assisted by the best military leader in the family, his younger brother John, Lord Montagu. Lancastrian opposition was centred on the Northumbrian castles of Alnwick, Bamburgh and Dunstanburgh. Warwick took the castles in September 1461 and again in the following year. On both occasions Edward IV, as part of his general policy of conciliation, restored the castles to their Lancastrian lords. However, men like Somerset and Sir Ralph Percy were intractable Lancastrians. By spring 1463 they and the county of Northumberland were in rebellion again.

Edward's diplomacy proved more fruitful than his policy of conciliation. Margaret of Anjou had successfully sought support from France and Scotland. However, Edward was able to arrange truces with both countries in October and December 1463 respectively. The Lancastrians found themselves isolated in their Northumbrian strongholds. Their attempt to disrupt further Yorkist–Scottish negotiations ended in disaster when Montagu routed a Lancastrian force at Hedgeley Moor in April 1464. Sir Ralph Percy was killed, dealing a serious blow to Lancastrian loyalties in the north. Montagu followed up his victory by defeating the main Lancastrian army at Hexham in May. Nearly all the remaining Lancastrian nobles were captured, and left to their own devices the Nevilles showed no mercy to their enemies. Amongst those executed was the Duke of Somerset. Warwick successfully besieged the Northumbrian castles, using his artillery to devastating effect on Bamburgh, and all resistance in the north collapsed. In Wales Sir William Herbert performed a similar task and established Yorkist control. Only Harlech Castle held out as a forlorn Lancastrian stronghold until August 1468. What seemed to be the final blow to Lancastrian fortunes came with the capture of Henry VI in Lancashire in 1465.

Despite his policy of conciliation, Edward IV relied on a comparatively small group of men from the beginning of his reign. These men were the principal beneficiaries in the large-scale distribution of titles, offices and estates that followed the attainting for treason of thirteen peers and many other Lancastrians in the Parliament of 1461. In the twenty-one years of his reign Edward created or revived at least thirty-five peerage titles – namely four dukes, two marquises, eleven earls, two viscounts and sixteen barons (**81**, p. 90). The vast majority of these were made in the course of the first reign, particularly in the first few years. Edward's generosity to Warwick set his rewards in a class of their own (see pp. 58–9), but other members of the Neville family also benefited. For example, Montagu was rewarded for his services in the north by being made Earl of Northumberland in 1464.

Edward also endowed his own brothers. George was created Duke of Clarence, an obvious evocation of the Yorkist claim to the throne from Lionel of Clarence, and Richard Duke of Gloucester. In addition to his brothers and the Nevilles, Edward relied on a group of about a dozen nobles, the majority of whom were his own creations (**54**, pp. 72–3). The most important of these men had previous Yorkist connections and became Edward's most trusted advisers.

None stood closer to the King than his chamberlain, Sir William Hastings. He was given extensive estates in the midlands centred on Leicestershire, formerly a strong Lancastrian area (**54**, pp. 73–5). The rise of Sir William Herbert was even more dramatic. In return for his services in Wales, this very ambitious and grasping Welsh squire was transformed into a prominent noble with an annual income of some £2,400 (**81**, p. 92).

Herbert's position in Wales compares with that of the Nevilles in the north. This policy of delegating local authority to powerful but trusted supporters was adopted by Edward in other trouble-spots. In the south-west responsibility was given firstly to the Neville Earl of Kent and then to Humphrey Stafford. Other members of the Yorkist nobility, established magnates like Henry Bourchier and Sir John Tiptoft and new creations such as Sir John Howard, served primarily at the centre of government (**54**, pp. 75–81). What jeopardised Edward's position and ultimately destroyed his dynasty were splits in this Yorkist nobility. The personalities and positions of Warwick and Herbert made their intense rivalry almost inevitable. Both were ruthlessly self-seeking and grasping. Warwick had long had designs on Wales. His feud with Edmund, Duke of Somerset, had been over the lordship of Glamorgan (see pp. 23–4). Once again he seemed to have been denied control of Wales. Warwick fell out with Herbert as early as 1461 over the lordship of Newport, and their ever-worsening rivalry was one of the principal causes of the renewal of civil war in 1469. By that date the strains in the Yorkist nobility had been greatly intensified by the appearance of the Woodville family.

Edward's marriage was of the greatest political and diplomatic importance. Warwick realised this and sought firstly a Scottish match and then a French one. However, on May Day 1464, under conditions of the greatest secrecy, Edward married Elizabeth Woodville, the impoverished widow of the Lancastrian Sir John Grey, who had been killed at St Albans in 1461 [**doc. 17**]. It is very difficult to fathom any political motive for the marriage. Edward scarcely needed to marry Elizabeth Woodville to assert his independence from Warwick. It was in character that he might impulsively marry her to obtain her favours. The consequences of the marriage are examined below (see pp. 59–60), but it was certainly a mistake. Elizabeth had little to recommend her except her physical beauty. She was devious and intensely ambitious for her family.

Edward's long delay in announcing the marriage shows his appreciation of its shortcomings. He was finally forced by the pressure of Warwick's diplomacy to divulge his marriage to the great Council at Reading in September 1464. Warwick had been negotiating a French marriage and was due to go to a conference at St Omer in October. It was this which forced Edward's hand at Reading. The nobles, and above all Warwick, can only have been astonished and then angered at Edward's failure to consult them, as was customary on so important an issue. However, they had no choice but to accept the *fait accompli*, though their confidence in the King's judgement must have been badly shaken. Warwick can only have resented the way he had been made to look a fool in the eyes of Louis XI of France, and indeed the marriage did signal a decline in his influence over the King. Edward was not the sort of man to compromise his authority. He was no-one's puppet. His direction of policy served to widen the rift between himself and Warwick. This was not intentional but perhaps inevitable given the personalities of the men involved. Edward actively promoted his wife's family through a series of advantageous marriages which gave offence to Warwick (see p. 59); but the greatest blow to the Earl's overweening pride was in the field of foreign policy.

The revival of England under Edward IV made her a vital factor in the rivalry of Louis XI and Duke Charles the Bold of Burgundy. Both actively sought an English alliance. Despite the collapse of his marriage plans – the conference at St Omer was never held – Warwick still strongly advocated a French alliance. Against him were the Woodvilles and much more importantly English commercial interests – Burgundy was the country's most important cloth market – and the patriotic sentiments of the people. Edward was always a good judge of opinion and particularly that of the London merchants. A commercial treaty was drawn up between England and Burgundy in November 1467, followed by a marriage treaty in spring 1468. Charles the Bold was married to Edward's sister, Margaret of York. However, very little came from the alliance. Louis XI responded by stirring up trouble in Wales, but it was crushed by Herbert. A far greater danger to Edward lay in the north – a sulking Warwick, his pride and ego badly hurt.

6 Rebellions and the Readeption* of Henry VI 1469–1471

The accession of Edward IV had done little to improve law and order in England. The troubles in the north and Wales were eventually overcome, but the general effectiveness of the law in the 1460s must remain very questionable. There was certainly a disturbing decline in law and order at the end of the decade. Even allowing for the problems of maintaining internal peace in the fifteenth century, the King's own 'supporters' were a principal factor in this decline. There were complaints concerning the abuse of local justice by members of the Yorkist nobility. The feuds of some were breaking out into violence [**doc. 18**]. Above all, there was the disorder inspired by the disaffection of the Earl of Warwick.

Edward sought conciliation with Warwick, but he would not compromise his policies. In January 1468 Warwick appeared before the King and the Council at Coventry. He went through a 'reconciliation' with Herbert and several other prominent Yorkists, but not with the Woodvilles. On foreign policy he would not give an inch and urged the King to abandon such self-interested rulers as the Duke of Burgundy (**54**, p. 118). The harmony between Edward and Warwick in the early months of 1468 was merely the cover for the latter's plotting. He found a willing confederate in Clarence, an ambitious, jealous and generally unstable character, who had no obvious reasons for discontent other than personal greed. Edward had endowed him with lands valued at £3,666 per annum and various offices which brought in a further 1,000 marks. His only grievance against Edward was the King's refusal to sanction his proposed marriage to Isabel Neville, but it hardly justified rebellion. Clarence wanted more patronage, more lands and more influence at court. In his mind the Woodvilles were denying him these 'rights', so he allied with their enemy, Warwick.

The internal state of the country deteriorated further in late 1468. Warwick set about exploiting the resultant popular discontent to his own ends. He was using the Duke of York's strategy of the 1450s against York's own son. In contrast to the King, Warwick, partly due to his generosity to local populations wherever he went, remained very popular. However, his support amongst the nobility was altogether a different matter. The crisis for Edward began in April 1469 with the rising led by Robin of Redesdale in Yorkshire. It appears to have been dispersed by Montagu, but the rebels regrouped in Lancashire. Another movement sprang up under a leader called Robin of Holderness in the East Riding but this was also suppressed by Montagu. The former rising was almost certainly inspired by Warwick, as Redesdale was probably Sir John Conyers, the Earl's retainer and cousin by marriage, but it also drew strongly on popular discontent.

Edward reacted to the threat in a very leisurely manner. Early in July 1469 he reached Newark where he received disturbing reports on the scale of the revolt and therefore fell back to Nottingham to await reinforcements from Wales. Meanwhile Warwick and Clarence had acted. They crossed to Calais, where Clarence and Isabel were married. The rebels also issued a manifesto stating their intention of reforming a government which was dominated by evil advisers. All the country's ills were laid at the door of their enemies amongst the Yorkist nobility. When Warwick and Clarence returned to Kent they attracted much support. What followed was a complete triumph for the rebels. Warwick intercepted Herbert and his supporters coming from Wales and defeated them at the battle of Edgecote (26 July 1469). Herbert was captured and executed. Several of the other 'evil' advisers suffered a similar fate. Warwick's triumph was sealed by the capture of Edward IV at Olney in Bedfordshire. However, as Warwick was to learn again in 1470–1, it was one matter to gain power, another to keep it.

Warwick's problems in power always centred on the attitude of the nobility. He triumphed in the summer of 1469 without any significant support amongst the nobility, and he did not have any large fund of patronage with which to purchase it. Warwick's 'reign' soon collapsed amidst local disorders. He was forced to release Edward from captivity and use his authority to crush a Lancastrian rising on the northern borders. Edward seized his opportunity and summoning his surviving supporters returned to London in October 1469. Despite Edward's initial desire for revenge, the loss of many of his principal supporters dictated a policy of conciliation. Edward, Warwick and Clarence went through a public show of reconciliation and a general pardon was issued for all offences committed before Christmas. However, that was the extent of the concessions. An uneasy peace ensued.

Warwick's brief triumph in the summer of 1469 had achieved

little beyond the death of several of his enemies. He had not re-established himself as the King's principal adviser. His actions in 1470 reveal an increasing sense of desperation. Warwick probably planned to put Clarence on the throne, but Edward was now on his guard. The King reacted quickly to the rebellion inspired by Warwick and Clarence in Lincolnshire and routed the insurgents at 'Lose-coat Field' near Stamford in March 1470. The rebellion attracted little real support and even some of Warwick's and Clarence's retainers failed to turn out. Warwick and Clarence had little choice but to flee. They were refused entry to Calais by Warwick's own deputy, Lord Wenlock, and in May they landed in the kingdom of France.

Warwick's arrival in France provided Louis XI with an opportunity to implement his plan for a Neville–Lancastrian alliance to restore Henry VI. This would give him an English alliance against Burgundy. It took all Louis's considerable powers of persuasion to arrange this remarkable alliance, but Warwick and Margaret of Anjou finally came to an agreement at Angers in July 1470 [**doc. 19**]. Its central feature was the betrothal of Prince Edward to Warwick's younger daughter, Anne. Plans were laid for an invasion of England, but Margaret refused to risk her precious son until Henry VI was finally back on the throne. Edward IV was not unaware of these momentous happenings in France but he found himself isolated when Warwick landed in Devon in September 1470. A storm had dispersed the defending royal fleet and to make matters worse Edward was in the north suppressing a rebellion inspired by Lord FitzHugh, Warwick's brother-in-law.

Edward came south but his position was rendered hopeless by the sudden and unexpected defection of Montagu to Warwick. Montagu's action is relatively easy to explain. In March 1470 Edward had restored Henry Percy to his father's forfeited earldom of Northumberland. Montagu was compensated by being made a marquis and having his son betrothed to Edward's daughter, but he still lost lands and the eastern wardenship to Henry Percy. Neither was he given Warwick's northern estates after the Earl's flight to France in May. Given Montagu's defection, Edward was left with little option but to seek refuge abroad. In early October he and his principal supporters, including Gloucester, Hastings and Earl Rivers, took ship for Burgundy. The remainder of the nobility remained in England and acquiesced in the new regime of Henry VI and the Earl of Warwick.

Despite his bloodless victory, Warwick's position was extremely precarious. The Readeption government depended upon an uneasy alliance between Warwick, Clarence and their followers, the Lancastrians, and the moderate, largely Yorkist nobility who had remained behind. The presence of the latter dictated a policy of conciliation and only the highly unpopular Constable of England, Sir John Tiptoft, was attainted and executed. Once again Warwick had no great fund of land or offices with which to reward his supporters or buy new support. The majority of the nobility were unsympathetic, if not actively hostile to the new government. Many were creations of Edward IV, and could only feel apprehension at the future. When the exiled Lancastrian leaders returned, they were bound to claim their forfeited lands which this new nobility now held. Clarence fell into this bracket. He had gained little from the restoration of Henry VI and despite the promise of compensation for the return of his estates to the Lancastrians, there was no likelihood of him receiving it. There was really just not enough land to satisfy everybody.

The return of the Lancastrians hardly promised much more for Warwick. Margaret of Anjou and Prince Edward would inevitably replace the beleaguered Earl as the power behind Henry VI. Popular opinion was on the side of Warwick but precious little else. He pressed ahead with his commitment to Louis XI to go to war with Burgundy and commanded the Calais garrison to begin the campaign in February 1471 [**doc. 20**]. Warwick's decision on war with Burgundy had disastrous consequences. The London merchants turned against the government and refused to furnish any loans. It also strained Warwick's uneasy alliance with the Lancastrians, some of whom, notably the Dukes of Somerset and Exeter, wanted to come to an agreement with Charles the Bold in an effort to isolate Edward IV. The greatest effect was upon Charles the Bold himself.

The actions of Louis XI and Warwick forced Charles into helping the exiled Yorkists. For two months he had professed friendship for Henry VI, hoping to avoid war with France, but early in 1471 he gave secret aid to the Yorkists. Edward had already been in contact with Clarence and other potential supporters, including the Earl of Northumberland. In March Edward set sail for England with 1,200 men and 36 ships. Warwick had made extensive preparations against the Yorkists. The Earl of Oxford effectively controlled East Anglia and therefore Edward decided against a landing at Cromer. Instead he sailed north and landed at Ravenspur on 14 March. Yorkshire proved hostile so Edward said that he had returned to claim his inheritance, not the crown, and donned an ostrich feather, the livery of Prince Edward, as proof of his loyalty. These measures gained him time and he was allowed to enter York, but only with a handful of men. Edward was not receiving much support but neither was he encountering much opposition. Both Montagu and Northumberland adopted a policy of 'wait and see'. The value of the latter's restoration was now apparent.

Edward pushed south and at last began to receive major support. At Leicester 3,000 men joined him from Hasting's affinity. His position was still precarious, since he was surrounded by hostile forces: Montagu to the north, Oxford to the east and Warwick to the south. However, Edward was at his best in 1471. He prevented his enemies uniting by marching rapidly to besiege Warwick in Coventry. This gave Clarence his chance to defect to his brother in early April 1471. Clarence tried to reconcile Edward and Warwick but failed, probably due to the latter's intransigence.

Clarence's defection fatally weakened Warwick's cause, and after some hesitation the Londoners admitted Edward IV in triumph to the city on 11 April. Henry VI was placed in the Tower. Edward raised an army and advanced to meet the Neville–Lancastrian forces at Barnet on Easter Sunday, 14 April 1471. He won a great victory in which Warwick and Montagu were killed. Oxford fled to Scotland. On the same day Margaret of Anjou and Prince Edward landed at Weymouth. They were joined by Somerset and received considerable support in the south-west but they were facing an inspired Edward. He raised fresh troops and marched rapidly across England to confront the Lancastrians at Tewkesbury on 4 May. The battle resulted in another great Yorkist victory. Prince Edward was killed and Somerset and many other leading Lancastrians were executed. Margaret was taken into captivity.

7 The Second Reign of Edward IV 1471–1483

Edward IV regained his kingdom through his determination, energy and military ability. The basis of his success was the greater noble support he was able to command. The noble retinues contained the most professional fighting men, more than offsetting the numerical superiority of the Nevilles and Lancastrians. There was a general collapse of resistance after the Lancastrian defeat at Tewkesbury, though London did suffer a short siege by the Kentishmen. Edward's approach signalled the end of the siege and he entered the city in triumph on 21 May 1471. On the same night Henry VI died in the Tower. It was far too convenient to be anything save murder, a view confirmed by the exhumation of the body in 1910. Gloucester, as Constable of the Tower, has often borne the blame, but ultimate responsibility clearly lay with Edward [**doc. 21**]. The Lancastrians were now entirely eliminated in the male line. The only remnant of their cause was Margaret Beaufort's son Henry Tudor, who was in exile. His future looked extremely bleak, for the Yorkist dynasty appeared to be firmly established.

However, the second reign of Edward IV was not without its problems. These largely centred on the royal family and the Woodvilles. After his restoration in 1471, Edward was careful to keep a tight control over his noble creations and royal patronage (**81**, pp. 93–4). The principal beneficiaries were members of the royal family and above all his youngest brother, the Duke of Gloucester. In July 1471 Gloucester was granted all of Warwick's estates north of the Trent. He also resumed the office of warden of the western March which had been granted to him in 1470. Gloucester's power in the north was further increased during the course of the second reign (**56**, pp. 24–26).

In contrast to Gloucester, Clarence had possessed extensive estates before 1470. They were restored and added to by Edward in a remarkable show of generosity in 1471. Clarence was given the Courtenay lands in compensation for his former Percy estates which had reverted to the Earl of Northumberland. Considering his record of treason, Clarence had more than landed on his feet, but he was still not satisfied. In particular he resented the grant of Warwick's northern lands to Gloucester. As a conciliatory move Edward revoked the grant of Richmond to Gloucester and regranted it to Clarence. The rivalry between the two brothers surfaced again when Clarence learnt that Gloucester wished to marry the widowed Anne Neville. In terms of both birth and wealth, Anne was the obvious bride for Gloucester. The marriage would enable him to secure her share of the Warwick inheritance. Neither brother emerges with much credit from this sordid scramble for lands at the expense of the rights of Warwick's widow. Clarence was more petulant and unaccommodating but both brothers exhibited a ruthless greed for land.

Clarence's anger is easily explained. He had hoped to inherit the Beauchamp–Despenser estates through his wife, Isabel. If Gloucester married Isabel's sister then his inheritance of these estates might be in jeopardy. Clarence went to extraordinary lengths to prevent the marriage, possibly even hiding Anne as a kitchenmaid in his London residence. However, Gloucester was not going to be denied. He sought her out and they were probably married after Easter 1472. The quarrel had already become public before the marriage, and Edward had no choice but to intervene. The two brothers were summoned to put their case before the royal Council at the palace of Sheen in February 1472. Edward forced a settlement but one very much in Clarence's favour. Clarence was confirmed in his possession of all the Neville estates he held except those already granted to Gloucester in the north. His seniority would seem to be implied by his creation as Earl of Warwick and Salisbury in March 1472 [**doc. 22**].

However, the feud rumbled on. Both Clarence and Gloucester wished to hold their Neville estates by inheritance, which meant extinguishing the claims of Warwick's widow. Neither had Clarence really reconciled himself to having only a share of the Neville estates. Edward continued to try to placate him and in May 1472 Gloucester was forced to resign the office of Great Chamberlain of England in favour of Clarence. In the following month, Gloucester persuaded his mother-in-law to leave sanctuary at Beaulieu in Hampshire and join her daughter in the north. It was rumoured that she intended to give all the Neville estates to the attentive Gloucester. It was left to Edward once again to intervene. In November 1473 Parliament passed an act of Resumption*, the fourth of the reign. Clarence was not exempted and was thus deprived of all the estates he held by royal grant. This salutary reminder of royal power was followed by a further act of Parliament in May 1474 which settled all the Neville estates on Clarence and Gloucester in right of their wives. The claim of Warwick's widow was pronounced legally void. Thus Edward used his control of Parliament to pass acts which supported claims to land untenable in any court of common law (**56**, pp. 26–31).

Clarence had seemingly done well out of the whole affair, but he was still not contented. His greed seems to have known no bounds. He undoubtedly resented the growing regional power of Gloucester in the north and the Woodvilles in Wales. In December 1476 his wife died at Warwick. As heirs he only had a son less than two years old and a daughter not yet four, so he needed a young wife of correct social standing. There was a lack of any suitable candidates in England, so Clarence looked abroad and decided on Charles the Bold's daughter, Mary of Burgundy. Edward refused to allow the marriage. It could well have involved him in a costly military alliance to defend a Burgundy reeling from the death of Mary's father at the battle of Nancy in January 1477. It would also endanger the terms of the Treaty of Picquigny with France (see p. 73), the preservation of which dominated Edward's foreign policy. However, these considerations were probably secondary to the King's personal motives. He not surprisingly distrusted Clarence and thought a Burgundian alliance might fuel his insatiable ambition. Edward also vetoed a Scottish match, presumably for the same reasons (**39**, pp. 130–133).

With his resentment growing and his ambitions thwarted, Clarence began to lose his self-control. In April 1477 he kidnapped, convicted and executed a former attendant, Ankarette Twynyho, for poisoning his wife, and one John Thursby for 'murdering' his infant son Richard. The charges were ridiculous. Edward kept his patience, but not for long. He was not going to tolerate any more blatant abuses of justice. Clarence may well have been involved in a rising in Cambridgeshire in the summer of 1477. At the same time John Stacey and Thomas Burdett, the latter a member of Clarence's household, were found guilty and hanged at Tyburn for plotting the King's death. Clarence protested that they had been convicted in error, calling into question the processes of the law. Edward reacted by imprisoning him in the Tower.

In January 1478 Clarence was arraigned before Parliament on a charge of high treason. He denied all the accusations but no-one spoke in his defence. Edward provided the evidence against him and Parliament found him guilty. He was executed – according to tradition, by drowning in a butt of Malmesey wine – in the Tower on 18 February 1478. The responsibility lay with the King who had evidently had enough of Clarence's conspiring and discontent. The Parliament was tightly controlled in both its personnel and its actions. However, behind Edward lay the influence of the Woodvilles. According to one contemporary account the Queen feared that Clarence was conspiring against the succession of Edward IV's son, Prince Edward [**doc. 23**]. There is no contemporary evidence to support the later charge that Gloucester engineered Clarence's downfall, but Edward must have consulted him and Gloucester must have acquiesced in the decision. He certainly gained far from negligible offices and estates in the aftermath of Clarence's fall (**56**, pp. 33–4).

After 1478 Gloucester spent less and less time at court. This and the death of Clarence greatly increased the influence of the Woodville family. Indeed it was a major blunder of the King to allow them even greater freedom for their ambitions in the second reign. They established a regional hegemony in Wales by exploiting the patronage and resources vested in Edward's two sons, who were firmly under their control at Ludlow Castle. The rise of the Woodvilles in these years was not achieved without alienating several noble families. In aggrandising his sons and the Woodvilles, Edward once again acted without due regard to the right of inheritance. The Herbert family was forced to give up the earldom of Pembroke in 1479, receiving only that of Huntingdon in compensation. They also lost their power and offices in south Wales. The co-heirs to the Mowbray inheritance – William, Lord Berkeley, and John, Lord Howard – lost out to Edward's younger son, Richard, who was given the formal succession to the inheritance. Another who felt resentment was Henry, Duke of Buckingham, who had been forced to marry a Woodville and yet still found himself excluded from power and influence at court [**doc. 24**].

Edward's closest adviser, Lord Hastings, was also on bad terms with the Woodvilles. The Queen probably resented his influence over the King, while her brother Earl Rivers, had never forgiven Hastings for replacing him as Captain of Calais in 1471. Hastings had also quarrelled with the Queen's son by her first marriage, the Marquis of Dorset. The Yorkist nobility was thus deeply divided. Above all, there was a conflict inherent in the positions and power of the Woodvilles and the Duke of Gloucester (**56**, pp 34–40).

8 The Reign of Edward V April–June 1483

Richard, Duke of Gloucester, gave loyal and devoted service to Edward IV. He brought effective law and order to the north and led the English forces in the war with Scotland (1480–2). He occupied Edinburgh and captured Berwick for the last time. To help Gloucester conduct the war, Edward had appointed him lieutenant-general in the north in May 1480, and as a reward for his service, he and his heirs were granted in January 1483 a great palatine comprising Cumberland and Westmorland and any adjacent parts of Scotland they might care to conquer. In this way Edward consciously built up his youngest brother into the most powerful northern baron in the middle ages. Surprisingly, Gloucester's rise did not unduly alienate the other leading nobles in the region – the Earl of Northumberland and Thomas, Lord Stanley. His general predominance in the area was reflected in the large number of private disputes submitted to his jurisdiction.

The Woodvilles were jealous of Gloucester, but above all they feared his power. Gloucester probably resented their influence over the King and at court. He seldom came to London and was in the north when Edward fell ill at Easter 1483. The King died on Wednesday 9 April. Edward was aware of the divisions his policies had created within the nobility, but he had not counted on his premature death while his son was still a minor. He attempted a death-bed reconciliation between Hastings and Dorset, but although they went through a show of mutual affection, it counted for nothing. Edward's premature death removed all restraint and a ruthless power struggle ensued which ultimately destroyed the Yorkist dynasty. Many weaker and less successful kings secured the safe succession of their sons, but Edward IV failed in this crucial test of medieval kingship.

Edward's will has not survived but it would seem certain that Gloucester, the only remaining adult male in the royal line, was made Protector. There was no real alternative, as the nobility were not prepared to accept the Woodvilles. Equally the Woodvilles were not going to allow anyone to wrest control of the princes from them.

They were determined to maintain their position by overthrowing the provisions of the will. The family were well positioned to do just that. Rivers was at Ludlow with the young King and possessed the power to raise an army in Wales. The rest of the family were in London where Dorset, as deputy Constable of the Tower, controlled the treasure. The Woodvilles were also strongly represented on the Council, which they hoped to use to defeat Gloucester's claim to power in a minority government. They very nearly succeeded. The Council proceeded to reject the will, preferring that, as in 1422, power should reside in a Minority Council with Gloucester as chief councillor [**doc. 24**]. There was another important precedent from the reign of Henry VI. Humphrey of Gloucester's protectorate had ended at Henry's coronation. Therefore the Woodvilles wished to crown Edward V as quickly as possible. Without waiting for the arrival of Gloucester, the Council set an early date for the coronation, Sunday 4 May.

However, opposition to the naked ambition of the Woodvilles was beginning to appear. Its inspiration was Lord Hastings. He and his friends argued that by blood the Woodvilles were unfitted to make such important decisions. There followed a furious row in the Council, with Hastings and his supporters opposing the Woodville plan to bring the King to London with an army. It was finally agreed that the escort should be limited to 2,000 men. Meanwhile Dorset was using the royal treasure to equip a fleet under Sir Edward Woodville.

No official letter seems to have been sent to Gloucester telling him of his brother's death. It appears to have been Hastings who informed him and urged him to come to London to protect his rights under the will [**doc. 24**]. Gloucester was not without support. It came from families who had suffered from the rise of the Woodvilles and Edward IV's arbitrary disregard for the rights of inheritance (see p. 41). Gloucester probably did not learn of Edward's death until some ten days after it took place. He wrote letters of condolence to the Queen and another to the Council, expressing his willingness to undertake the protectorate. This seems to have put the Woodvilles off their guard and they dropped their emphasis on the urgency of getting the King to London as quickly as possible. Rivers certainly seems to have believed in Gloucester's good intentions, for he arranged to meet him with the King on their way to the capital.

After a solemn memorial service for the dead King at York, where the northern nobility swore an oath of allegiance to Edward V, Gloucester set off for London with a large retinue. He arrived at

Northampton on 29 April where he met by arrangement the Duke of Buckingham with a force of some 300 men [**doc. 24**]. Rivers and the King were fourteen miles nearer the capital at Stony Stratford. In order to greet Gloucester, Rivers and his nephew Sir Richard Grey rode back to Northampton. Gloucester entertained his guests that evening and arrested them on the following morning. He and Buckingham then moved on to Stony Stratford where they took possession of the young King. Sir Thomas Vaughan and other principal members of the royal household were arrested and sent with Rivers and Grey to Gloucester's strongholds in the north. The news of events at Stony Stratford threw the Woodvilles in London into utter confusion. Dorset tried to raise an army but failed and then fled to join the Queen and her other son Richard, Duke of York, in sanctuary at Westminster. With them went the remainder of the treasure; indeed the sanctuary wall had to be enlarged to get it all in.

Against a background of rumour, unease and suspicion, Gloucester, Buckingham and Edward V entered London on 4 May [**doc. 24**]. The Council immediately confirmed Gloucester's position as Protector and accorded him greater powers than his father had exercised in his protectorates in the 1450s. However, Gloucester was unable to persuade the Council that Rivers and his associates should be attainted for treason, though he went ahead and treated their lands as forfeit. This was a clear sign that the Council would only back Gloucester as long as he promoted the succession of Edward V. A new date, Sunday 22 June, was set for the coronation. This posed a real problem for Gloucester, as his protectorate was thus limited to a period of weeks. The accession of a king, educated and influenced by the Woodvilles, would inevitably lead to a revival of Woodville power.

Gloucester seems to have initially thought of extending the protectorate beyond the coronation (**56**, p. 75). Meanwhile he consolidated his position by exercising the powers of appointment and patronage vested in him by virtue of his office. The greatest beneficiary was Buckingham, who was made Chief Justice and Chamberlain in both north and south Wales for life and given the authority to array men in the west country. He was also granted control of all the royal castles and lordships in Wales and the Marches. In this way Buckingham came to exercise an even greater authority in Wales than Herbert had during the first reign of Edward IV. Other beneficiaries included the Earl of Northumberland and Lord Howard. It is also clear that former officials and servants of Edward IV benefited. They of course remained loyal to Edward V but their co-operation with the Protector is sufficient to prove that there was no general belief, at this point in time, that Gloucester aimed to take the throne. The only group to suffer were the Woodvilles and their associates.

By the beginning of June, contemporary observers were in little doubt that Gloucester was planning to take the crown [**doc. 24**]. There seems no real evidence to dispute this. Gloucester, like his brother Edward IV, had shown himself to be ruthless in the defence of his interests and power. They had both ridden roughshod over the right of inheritance in the past, and Gloucester was prepared to do so again to preserve his position in the face of an uncertain future under a Woodville-indoctrinated king. Since Edward V was now twelve, Gloucester's protectorate, even if it was extended, could not possibly last longer than three or four years. He would then be exposed to the revenge of the Woodvilles, a family not renowned for compassion. It was in order to avert this threat that Gloucester seized the throne.

In early June Gloucester ordered military reinforcements to be sent urgently to him from the north, but in the event they did not reach London until July, by which time everything was over barring the coronation. Gloucester, Buckingham and Howard evidently had sufficient men to control the city, a crucial factor in the coming days. It seems unlikely that Hastings, suspecting Gloucester's intentions, had been in contact with the Woodvilles. Gloucester probably invented the story to justify his actions, for Hastings was bound to oppose his designs on the crown. On 13 June Gloucester acted and took his enemies completely by surprise. At the famous Council meeting held in the Tower he arrested Hastings, Lord Stanley and John Morton, Bishop of Ely, on charges of treason against the Protector and the government. Hastings was immediately beheaded, Morton imprisoned and Stanley later released [**doc. 24**].

The events of 13 June spread fear and dismay in the capital. Gloucester now moved rapidly to the crown. On 16 June the Archbishop of Canterbury, backed by a large number of armed men, persuaded the Queen to allow the Duke of York to leave sanctuary at Westminster for his brother's coronation. York joined his elder brother in the Tower. With both princes in his power, Gloucester presented his own claim. On 22 June, the day originally set for Edward V's coronation, Dr Ralph Shaw preached the rightful title of Gloucester to the crown at St Paul's Cross. He was followed two days later by Buckingham, who eloquently addressed the mayor and citizens of London on the same theme [**doc. 24**]. The nature of Gloucester's claim has been the subject of some debate. According to one account Edward IV was declared to have been a bastard – which does not say much for Gloucester's regard for his mother – while the other sources record that Edward's sons were pronounced illegitimate due to his pre-contract of marriage to Lady Eleanor Butler. Both claims are highly implausible and can be dismissed as mere propaganda to justify Gloucester's usurpation. The only other possible claimant was Clarence's son and heir, but he was firmly under Gloucester's control and excluded from the succession on the grounds of his father's attainder for treason.

Meanwhile orders had been sent north for the execution of Rivers, Grey and Vaughan. They were duly beheaded at Pontefract on 25 June. On the same day representatives of the three estates met at Westminster and examined the charges against Edward IV and then, largely out of fear, petitioned Gloucester to take the throne. After token hesitation, he accepted and the reign of Richard III commenced on 26 June 1483.

9 The Reign of Richard III 1483–1485

Richard was crowned on 6 July 1483. It was an ostentatious coronation but it heralded a short and unhappy reign. He had the best of intentions and proved to be an energetic and efficient king. His first act on taking the throne was to deliver a strict lecture to his judges in Westminster Hall on the impartial administration of justice to all his subjects. This of course was also good propaganda, drawing attention to the rather lax rule of Edward's later years. However, for all his attempts at 'good governance', Richard never escaped from the circumstances of his usurpation.

In mid-July Richard set off on a triumphal progress to present himself to his subjects. With an impressive entourage he passed along the Thames valley, up through the midlands and on to the north. According to the Bishop of St Davids he was greeted enthusiastically everywhere along his route, but the Bishop had close ties with Richard and was hardly impartial [**doc. 25**]. At the end of August Richard entered York in triumph, where his son and heir Edward was invested as Prince of Wales. In the middle of September the King began his journey back to London. When he reached Lincoln he received information from his effective intelligence network that the south and west was about to rebel under the Duke of Buckingham.

The origins of the rebellion are rather obscure but it seems a movement grew up in the south-east during August to rescue the princes before it was too late. The inspiration behind this movement probably came from the surviving Woodvilles. By September the dissent had spread, but in view of the widespread rumours of the death of the princes, the aim of the rebellion had turned into putting Henry Tudor on the throne. This was obviously the result of pressure from the other prime movers in the conspiracy, Margaret Beaufort and Bishop Morton. It was the latter, held in captivity by Buckingham, who involved the Duke in the rebellion, probably by exploiting his greed and distant claim to the throne. The principal conspirators were joined by substantial gentry in all the southern counties from Kent to Cornwall. Woodville influences and connections played a part, but the majority were loyal former officials and servants of Edward IV. It was not so much that they had lost their source of patronage as that they felt outraged by Richard's treatment of Edward's heirs (**56**, pp. 105–112).

The rebellion was a failure. Richard's spy network kept him well-informed about a movement whose security was very weak. The Kentish rising went off prematurely and was crushed by Howard, who happened to be in the south-east. Richard was therefore able to concentrate his resources against Buckingham, who found it difficult mustering his supporters and getting out of Wales. His men eventually dispersed of their own accord and Buckingham, betrayed by his own servants, was captured and executed without trial at Salisbury on 2 November. The rebellion had collapsed ignominiously. Henry Tudor appeared off the south-west coast but instead of landing sailed back to Brittany and exile, where he was joined by Morton, Dorset and a strong group of gentry leaders from the south and west.

Richard had crushed the rebellion relatively easily, but the serious advocacy of the previously obscure Henry Tudor and the attitude of the southern gentry were ominous developments. Richard III is unique amongst medieval English kings in the degree to which his power was based on a northern affinity (**56**, p. 44). However, he was an able politician and realised the necessity of creating wider-based support. Therefore as King he continued his policy as Protector and retained many of his brother's men in offices and distributed patronage to them. Yet it was these men who had rebelled in October 1483. Only in the aftermath of the rebellion did the northerners really come to the fore.

In the Parliament of January 1484, 104 persons were attainted for treason and their lands forfeited. About a third were later pardoned and recovered at least part of their estates but the remaining forfeitures were ruthlessly carried out. This enabled Richard to grant away revenues worth some £12,000 per annum. For reasons of trust and personal preference the bulk of these grants went to some forty northerners. They were mainly concentrated in the counties worst affected by the October rebellion, and where it was thought that Henry Tudor might return. Virtual control of local defence was placed in their hands, and in this way they took over the natural governing role of the local gentry and administrators. Their rule was viewed with great resentment as an attack on the rights of inheritance. The southern gentry regarded the northern intrusion as little short of tyranny (**79**). The most remarkable personification of this 'alien' rule was Sir Richard Ratcliffe, who was granted lands to the value of £650 per annum in Dorset, Somerset and Devon. However, it was not just northerners who benefited. William Catesby, Francis Lovel and Sir James Tyrell were all midlanders but still had very strong personal ties with Richard. The southern resentment found expression in Thomas Collingbourne's famous rhyme:

> The Cat, the Rat and Lovel our dog
> Rule all England under the Hog.

(The Cat was Catesby; the Rat Ratcliffe; while the Hog referred to Richard whose emblem was the white boar.)

At no time in his reign does Richard seem to have won the loyalty of the southern gentry. However, it does seem that he attracted support amongst the nobility. Many again were northerners, but others were won over by royal patronage and gave him loyal service. William Herbert, Earl of Huntingdon, and John de la Pole, Earl of Lincoln, fall into this category. He was equally successful amongst the lesser nobility. Again his northern affinity was at the heart of his support, but he also attracted a significant number of former associates of Edward IV – men like Lord Ferrers, Lord Cobham and Lord Grey of Codnor. It is a sign of Richard's success that no English peer declared for Tudor until the issue was settled at Bosworth (**56**, pp. 153–163).

However, Richard's position depended upon the loyalty of the heads of the four surviving great baronial families: Buckingham; Lord Howard, whom Richard created Duke of Norfolk; Lord Stanley; and the Earl of Northumberland. Buckingham was of course dead, but that merely enhanced the importance of the other three magnates. Howard received substantial patronage from Richard and, as Duke of Norfolk, came to dominate East Anglia. In return he served Richard as loyally as he had Edward IV. He played a crucial role in crushing Buckingham's rebellion and would die fighting for Richard at Bosworth. Lord Stanley and his family gained extensive estates in Wales and Cheshire after the rebellion of 1483, but their loyalty was always in doubt. Stanley was married to Margaret Beaufort and had been arrested and then, for reasons unknown, released in June 1483. The power of the Percy family had been eclipsed during the reign of Edward IV. The Earl supported Richard in 1483 but the new reign brought no major recovery of Percy power in the north. The eastern wardenship was granted only for short periods and an 'outsider', the Earl of Lincoln, was made president of the Council of the North (see p. 74). This probably explains the Earl's equivocal attitude at Bosworth (**56**; pp. 163–9).

In January 1484 Richard held the single Parliament of his reign. It is likely that the elections were strongly influenced in the royal interest and certainly Catesby was chosen as Speaker. Richard's title to the crown was ratified and the act of attainder against the rebels of 1483 was also accepted. His reforming legislation has received considerable attention and is discussed below (see p. 69). If the Parliament was a success, Richard was dealt a body-blow later in the year. In April his son and heir, Prince Edward, died at Middleham Castle. The death of Edward raised the spectre of another disputed succession, particularly as the delicate health of Queen Anne was deteriorating. She died in March of the following year.

Anne's death was followed by rumours that she had been poisoned by Richard, to enable him to marry his niece Elizabeth of York. These rumours illustrate perfectly contemporary suspicions and mistrust of the King. They became so widespread that Richard had to issue a public denial of the story. Richard's problems were compounded in the early months of 1485 by a shortage of money. In the Parliament he had declared benevolences* illegal, but Richard now resorted to forced loans which were scarcely any more popular, even though they were backed by pledges of repayment. Political considerations always took priority over the much-vaunted parliamentary legislation.

Richard needed the money to finance his preparations for the expected invasion by Henry Tudor. He had used fleets for national defence in 1483 and 1484 but he does not seem to have done so in the summer of 1485, probably due to his financial problems. Richard relied on his supporters, positioned at strategic positions along the coast, and his extensive intelligence network. He took up position in the centre of the country at Nottingham where he could quickly raise an army in response to any invasion.

Henry Tudor landed at Mill Bay in Milford Haven on 7 August 1485. South Wales was firmly held by the loyal families of Herbert and Vaughan, so Henry headed north. He was joined by Rhys ap Thomas, possibly after the promise of the 'perpetual lieutenantship of Wales' (**22** p. 217). Henry reached Shrewsbury by 15 August. All really depended on the attitude of the Stanleys. At Stafford, Henry met Lord Stanley's brother Sir William Stanley. Sir William probably pledged the family's support, but they did not openly join the rebel cause, for Richard was holding Lord Stanley's son, Lord Strange, as a hostage for the family's good behaviour.

Richard learnt of Henry's landing on 11 August and immediately summoned his nobles to muster their forces and join him at Leicester. Howard came from East Anglia and the Earl of Northumberland from the north, but the Stanleys acted in complete independence from the King. Richard seems to have received precious little support from the south and west but neither were they turning out for Henry. Many families were adopting a cautious stance of non-alignment, but this does not explain Richard's defeat.

Any reconstruction of the battle of Bosworth (22 August 1485) is a difficult task. The fullest account was written by a foreigner, Polydore Vergil, twenty years after the event, while the only significant contemporary account is very short. Nevertheless it is clear that Richard III, despite great personal bravery and skill in arms, lost the day and his crown due to that frequent decider of battles in the Wars of the Roses: treachery. The Earl of Northumberland, whether intentionally or not, took no part in the battle; but it was Sir William Stanley who decisively intervened on the side of Henry Tudor. Never again would the activities of such 'overmighty subjects' determine the future of the English crown.

Part Three: Assessment

10 Henry VI and the Lancastrian Dynasty

The weakness of Henry VI was the single most important factor in English politics in the middle years of the fifteenth century. Effective government in the later middle ages still largely depended on the ability of the monarch not only to reign but also to rule. As the scope and complexity of administration had grown, English kings had divested themselves of much of the routine of government to the burgeoning bureaucracy. Yet vital aspects of medieval rule, such as the direction of foreign policy, the distribution of patronage and relations with the nobility, remained the personal prerogative of the monarch. It was precisely in these areas of government that Henry VI most conspicuously failed.

The most vivid description of Henry VI is that penned by his former chaplain, John Blacman. He is portrayed as a very devout and kindly simpleton, preferring prayer to any practical aspects of kingship [**doc. 4**]. Serious doubts have recently been cast on the reliability of Blacman's account; even his authorship is now disputed. Blacman died in January 1485 whereas internal evidence points to the work being written in the later part of Henry VII's reign (**61**, pp. 5–6; **36**, pp. 3–4). There seems little doubt that Blacman's account was part of Henry VII's attempt to have Henry VI canonised. 'Saint' Henry is divorced from the disasters of his reign by being portrayed as a deeply pious, God-like figure, far above mere secular matters.

The contemporary evidence hardly supports such a divine interpretation of Henry VI. It is evident that even before the onset of his madness in 1453, his humbler subjects had a poor opinion of him. They regarded the King as simple-minded or dim-witted [**doc. 5**]. However, their view was based on the failure of his policies rather than any real perception of Henry's personality. Fortunately it is possible from surviving contemporary sources and also from his personal and political actions to get relatively close to the character of the last Lancastrian King. The principal characteristic associated with Henry is his extraordinary piety. The fifteenth century was an age of deep religious devotion and Henry was undoubtedly affected by this. He possessed a deep concern for the state of the Church and the ecclesiastical hierarchy. However, he does not appear to have been uniquely devoted to religious pursuits. Unlike his father he did not found a monastery or excessively endow chantries, nor did he do anything comparable to Henry V spending the whole night in prayer on the eve of his accession. Henry VI was a conventionally pious man in a pious age. His greatest (if not only) achievement was the foundation of the twin Colleges of Eton and King's, Cambridge, yet the cost of these was more a reflection of Henry's desire to outdo all similar foundations, particularly those of William of Wykeham, than of any sense of spiritual devotion.

Henry was very extravagant, whether in financing his foundations or his household. Contrary to the austere figure portrayed by Blacman, he spent freely on his gowns and hats. However, it was in the crucial art of patronage that Henry was most generous, and with disastrous consequences. He showed an almost naive lack of political judgement in surrounding himself with grasping, self-seeking and unpopular advisers and companions. It was a trait of his character that had worried his governor and tutor, Richard Beauchamp, Earl of Warwick, as early as 1432. Under Henry's rule, government became the prerogative of faction. He was deeply suspicious of any who criticised his rule, such as Gloucester and later York, and was capable of vindictive action against them. Society became increasingly fragmented under a king who failed to act as the essential unifying force in the country.

In stark contrast to his son, Henry V had not only maintained peace and stability at home but had also led England into glorious foreign adventures. He thus triumphantly succeeded in the two basic criteria of successful medieval kingship – the maintenance of internal law and order and the preservation of the integrity of the kingdom from external threat. The striking contrasts between the achievements of his short reign and the failures of the all too long reign of his inept son were only too obvious to contemporaries [**doc. 6**]. However, with hindsight, the viability of Henry V's conquests in France seems very doubtful. He profited from the internal divisions within a country inherently more powerful and wealthy than England. Therefore kings like Richard II and Henry VI who pursued a policy of peace might be credited with perceptive foresight. Richard seems to have appreciated the great strains war placed on the resources of the crown. Henry's motives for his peace policy are more difficult to fathom, though he was evidently uninterested in military matters. The basic problem for any late-medieval ruler wishing to pursue a policy of peace was the weight of contemporary opinion against it. War and its successful prosecution was almost a national institution – the Olympics or World Cup of the later middle ages. Henry was therefore flying in the face of public opinion, and to make matters a great deal worse, he mishandled his own peace policy. The nature and circumstances of the loss of France are solely attributable to Henry's government. He gave away Maine in December 1445, without negotiating any guarantees in return or informing his officers in France. He removed York and promoted the Beauforts, thereby throwing the command structure into confusion. Finally he authorised the attack on Fougères, which brought his peace policy down in ruins in the years 1449–1453. By 1450, Henry's faction-ridden government was thoroughly discredited.

In the final decade of Henry VI's reign, the Yorkists tried to perform the nobility's role, in the tradition of the Ordainers and the Appellants in the reigns of Edward II and Richard II respectively, of ridding the King and kingdom of grasping and unpopular advisers. The Duke of York had powerful personal reasons for assuming the leadership in this reform of government (see pp. 7–8, 20), but they all reflected his dynastic ambitions. York's repeated failures to impose himself as the King's leading adviser by constitutional means or military force led almost inevitably to his claim to the throne in October 1460. However, it is wrong to believe that the dynastic issue was only important in the Wars of the Roses after York's claim. There were major dynastic considerations behind many of the actions of Henry VI.

There had been no dynastic problems for the House of Lancaster in the reign of Henry V. The victor of Agincourt had three healthy brothers, in addition to his son. Henry's death, leaving a nine-month-old heir, made his surviving brothers, the Dukes of Bedford and Gloucester, dynastically very important. However, like the Duke of Clarence who was killed at the battle of Baugé in 1421, both Bedford and Gloucester died without a legitimate heir. The latter was wholly unacceptable to Henry VI anyway and the fear of his dynastic ambitions probably influenced the attack on his second wife, Eleanor Cobham, in 1441 and finally on Gloucester himself in 1447. The death of Gloucester left the Duke of York, the embodiment of the Mortimer claim, as heir presumptive. It can only have raised his ambitions for himself and his family which, in stark contrast to the Lancastrian line, was abundantly fertile. York's marriage to Cecily Neville produced four daughters and eight sons, of whom two were later to become kings of England.

The Mortimer claim dated back to 1399 and the usurpation of Henry of Lancaster. In taking the throne Henry IV had ignored the claim of the Mortimer line. This derived from Lionel of Clarence, the third son of Edward III; whereas Henry's father, John of Gaunt, was Edward's fourth son (see Genealogies, pp. 100–2). Henry IV concealed the weakness of his claim in a vague declaration alluding to his rights by blood and conquest, in the Parliament of September 1399 [**doc. 1**]. However, given the authority and support which Henry IV possessed in 1399, there was no feasible alternative to the House of Lancaster. The Mortimer claim failed to command any real support until the middle of the fifteenth century and Henry IV was succeeded by his son and, in due course, his grandson. Nevertheless the circumstances of 1399 did impose severe and ultimately fatal limitations on the new dynasty. Political opposition was made all the more dangerous by the mere presence of the Mortimer claim. Rebellions could be justified by attacking the title as well as the person of the monarch. Lancastrian stability depended upon continued political and military success and more fundamentally the character of the king. Incompetence and political failure were more than usually dangerous to the House of Lancaster.

The Lancastrians were only too well aware of the Mortimer claim. Some of the pedigrees drawn up for them in the 1430s and 1440s have survived, and they all exclude reference to the line of Lionel of Clarence. Many were later amended by the Yorkists to include it. Equally interesting is a specific pedigree for 1444 which includes the Beauforts, the Staffords and the Holands in the Lancastrian royal family. Henry VI's marriage to Margaret of Anjou was of the greatest importance in strengthening the dynasty, but it was only natural that the King should also turn to the junior branches of the royal family. It was these families – the Staffords, the Holands and primarily the Beauforts – who dominated Henry VI's government and household. The Beauforts were specifically debarred from the royal succession by statute in February 1407. Henry VI probably had hopes of annulling this statute and York no doubt feared that he would do so in favour of his great rival Edmund, Duke of Somerset. Members of all these families were given dukedoms in the mid 1440s, a title reserved for members of the royal family. In 1450 Margaret Beaufort, then barely seven years old, married the Duke of Suffolk's son and heir. Many contemporaries regarded this as a route to the throne for the hated de la Pole family and the whole affair demonstrated the great uncertainty surrounding the order of succession (**69**).

Assessment

The birth of Prince Edward in October 1453 merely exacerbated the underlying sense of dynasty in contemporary rivalries. Margaret of Anjou clearly regarded York as a dynastic threat to her ailing husband and the succession of her son, and as she came to dominate the household and government she determined on the destruction of the Yorkists. York responded by claiming the throne in 1460. This was a mistake, because of the cautious attitude of the nobles and their commitment to their oath of allegiance to Henry VI. Considering the disasters of the reign it is a remarkable testimony to the mystical and practical powers of fifteenth-century kingship.

11 Edward IV and the Earl of Warwick

'He may be seen as the supreme example of the overmighty subject whose end must be either to destroy or be destroyed' (**49**, p. 69). This perceptive remark was made about Thomas of Lancaster, the great rival of Edward II, but it is clearly applicable to Richard Neville, Earl of Warwick. There are strong parallels between the careers of the two men. Both Lancaster and Warwick were able to gain power but found it difficult to maintain their authority. They lacked the sovereignty and prestige of kingship and experienced difficulties in cultivating support amongst their fellow nobles.

The character of Warwick remains something of an enigma. There is no surviving portrait, effigy or even a detailed description of his appearance. The Rous Roll contains a line drawing of the Earl but the illustration is more concerned with heraldry than his physical appearance. Rous revealed his admiration for Warwick in the accompanying description:

> this noble earl was a knight of the Garter and he had all England at his leading and was feared and respected through many lands . . . his knightly acts had been so excellent that his noble and famous name could never be put from laudable memory (**20**, cap. 57).

However, Rous was hardly impartial. His view was determined by the size of the Earl's benefactions to the town and churches of Warwick. Moreover the work was constructed for the favour of the current Lord of Warwick, Richard III, whose Queen was the Earl's daughter.

There was nothing 'knightly' about a career which earned for Warwick the nickname of 'Kingmaker'. His whole character seems dominated by a ruthless greed and ambition for land and power. He would appear to have had the worst record in the fifteenth century, with the possible exception of Richard III, for settling private scores by violence and judicial murder. His execution of Herbert and the others after Edgecote had no legal justification, since they were not in arms against the King whom Warwick still acknowledged. He possessed great force of character and energy, but these characteristics seem to have been solely channelled into political activities. Warwick does not appear to have been a great builder, patron of the arts or religious founder. This might have been a matter of economics, for his large revenues may have been absorbed by his exceptional and continual need to cultivate political and military support. All the same he maintained a luxurious and extravagant household. Apparently any man who had 'any acquaintance' with his house could get as much meat 'sodden or roast' as he liked to take away. It was his hospitality, his naval prowess and his pithy turn of phrase which caught men's imaginations. He always attracted support as the champion of the 'common weal', but he espoused popular grievances as a means to his own self-aggrandisement.

In 1461 Warwick played the crucial role in Edward IV's usurpation. Some historians have interpreted this as the first example of his 'kingmaking' (**41**, p. 97). This view is based on foreign accounts, which were prone to exaggerate Warwick's influence (**54**, p. 63). In fact it was an alliance of mutual interests which triumphed in 1461, not a puppet and puppeteer. From the beginning Edward demonstrated a will-power, determination and energy which, though they ebbed on occasions, made him a king to be reckoned with [**doc. 16**]. Moreover it was the young King who possessed the substance of military ability, the Earl only the myth. Edward triumphed at Mortimer's Cross, Towton, Barnet and Tewkesbury; Warwick was defeated at St Albans and Barnet.

Warwick's support was invaluable to Edward but he was more than amply rewarded. He dominated the nobility as no magnate had since Thomas of Lancaster. His lands embraced the vast Beauchamp, Despenser, Montagu and Neville estates and substantial properties forfeited from the Percy and Clifford families (**81**, p. 89). He also held a whole series of offices, the most important of which were those of Captain of Calais, Constable of Dover Castle, Warden of the Cinque Ports, Admiral of England, Ireland and Aquitaine and Warden of both the eastern and western Marches (**54**, pp. 70–1). In the early years of his reign the comparatively inexperienced Edward allowed Warwick a great deal of freedom in undertaking these duties, particularly in tackling the Lancastrian threat in the north. It was Warwick's activity and independence, in sharp contrast to Edward's relative inactivity in the south, which gave foreigners the impression that the King reigned while the Earl ruled. It was a mistake Louis XI also made.

By any standards Warwick was exceptionally grasping. Despite his great wealth, he never seems to have been satisfied. Even before Edward's marriage, he had shown obvious dissatisfaction at the direction of royal patronage. Warwick evidently still had designs on Wales and soon fell out with Sir William Herbert (see p. 31). He also fell foul of other prominent members of the new Yorkist nobility such as Humphrey Stafford and Lord Audley. These were the old scores that Warwick settled after his victory at Edgecote. However, above all his other rivals were the Woodvilles.

Edward's control of patronage showed that he intended to rule his own kingdom. In other vital areas of medieval kingship, such as his marriage and foreign policy, for better or for worse he was going to make the decisions. If his marriage was 'the first major blunder of his political career', then his decision on a Burgundian alliance was far more in tune with the economic and patriotic requirements of his kingdom than Warwick's self-interested notions (**54**, p. 85).

Edward's marriage to Elizabeth Woodville was a major setback for Warwick, reflecting the decline in his influence over the King. He had not been consulted and had carried on the negotiations for a French marriage in total ignorance. It can only have hurt his grossly-inflated ego. The series of Woodville marriages that Edward initiated to provide for his wife's family gave even greater offence to Warwick. Edward's support in these marriages was crucial as it enabled the Woodvilles to outbid all competition in the marriage market. These royal inducements influenced many nobles to enter into Woodville marriages but they undoubtedly left a legacy of resentment. By the end of 1466, one of the Queen's sisters had become the wife of the Duke of Buckingham while four others had married the heirs of the Earls of Kent, Essex and Arundel and of Lord Herbert; as for her male relatives, her elder son had married the heiress to the Duke of Exeter and a brother had married the Dowager Duchess of Norfolk who was at least sixty-five years old (**74**, pp. 60–73).

Several of the marriages are said to have given direct offence to Warwick, but even more worrying for the Earl was the fact that they removed all likely candidates for his two daughters, Isabel and Anne. Warwick's plan to marry Isabel to Clarence was the logical consequence of the Woodville marriages. Edward's refusal to approve the match merely added to the Earl's grievances. However, at the root of Warwick's hatred of the Woodvilles was the belief that they had replaced him as the principal influence on the King. In the late 1460s Woodville influence was growing and that of Warwick waning. At court the Woodvilles associated with their marriage connections and the new Yorkist nobility. The most prominent of the latter was Herbert, who already had his own personal feud with Warwick over their ambitions in Wales.

The Woodville–Herbert alliance must have caused some alarm to Warwick. Herbert also exploited his influence at court to secure advantageous marriages. He even planned to secure the reversal of past attainders to supply his daughters' bridegrooms with magnate estates. These plans centred on the former lands of the Percy and Tudor families, which were currently held by Warwick and Clarence. He seems to have been oblivious to the likely repercussions. The decline of Warwick's influence was further marked by two royal decisions. In June 1467 his brother, Archbishop Neville, was dismissed as chancellor, and in a matter of months Edward had signed the Anglo-Burgundian alliance. These setbacks were the final humiliation for Warwick. He was already involved with Louis XI. Now he became trapped through his overweening pride and ambition in the diplomatic web of the arch-intriguer of Europe. His release only really came with his death at Barnet in 1471. It was an almost inevitable ending.

It is undoubtedly true that 'only undermighty kings have overmighty subjects'. Powerful men like Warwick, and before him Thomas of Lancaster, were able to pursue their apparently limitless ambitions in the 'undermighty' reigns of kings such as Henry VI and Edward II. However, the rule of Edward IV was a different matter. The first Yorkist king was far from 'undermighty' as Warwick found to his cost in the years after 1461. This is not to say that Edward drove Warwick to rebellion. The King's marriage and promotion of the Woodvilles were in retrospect grave errors but they were not intended to alienate Warwick. He wanted the Earl's friendship and advice but in the final analysis he was his own master. In no sense was he going to allow Warwick to dominate government. Warwick was just not prepared to accept this state of affairs.

12 Myth and Reality

War and society

> . . . the slaughter of men was immense: for besides the dukes, earls, barons and distinguished warriors who were cruelly slain, multitudes almost innumerable of the common people died of their wounds. Such was the state of the kingdom for nearly ten years.
>
> cited (**35**), p. 196.

The Benedictine monk who penned this sorry tale of carnage during the Wars of the Roses has found little support for his views amongst modern historians. Most have argued that the bulk of the English population was left untouched by the wars. Life largely went on as before.

The impression given by the Benedictine monk and several other contemporary writers was, however, subtly developed by sixteenth-century historians to produce the Tudor view of the fifteenth century. The inspiration behind this view was Polydore Vergil, a native of Urbino in Italy. He was already a humanist of international renown when he came to England in 1502, as a deputy of his patron, Cardinal Adriano Castelli, for the collection of papal revenue. Soon after his arrival he began work on the *Anglica Historia* following a formal request from Henry VII. The King would obviously welcome a defence of a dynasty whose claim to the throne was decidedly tenuous. However, it is a grave error to regard Vergil as merely a Tudor propagandist. The various offices he received in England were more the result of Castelli's influence with the King than of any direct royal patronage. His fortunes under Henry VIII were precarious in the extreme and for several months in 1515 he found himself imprisoned in the Tower due to a quarrel with Wolsey. The *Anglica Historia* was indeed dedicated to Henry VIII but such dedications were a common feature of the Renaissance. It was regarded as a positive necessity for kings to learn the lessons of history (**37**, pp. 126–7).

Nevertheless, Vergil clearly wrote within certain limitations. The Tudors obviously had to be presented in the best light and in his work all hopes are centred on Henry VIII. However, Vergil also sought after the truth, which he believed was the primary function of history. In his *Anglica Historia* Vergil produced a highly sophisticated account of England's history by applying humanist principles to a thorough examination of native sources, both literary and oral. He undoubtedly examined many contemporary accounts from the fifteenth century. In general these works are more concerned with political causes and events, but a few – like those of the Benedictine monk cited earlier, John Warkworth, Abbot Whethamstede of St Albans and John Hardyng – contain depressing accounts of widespread disorder and wholesale killings in the wars [**doc. 6**]. Some writers began to reflect on the unstable temperament of the English people. Vergil latched on to these accounts, presented their pessimistic view and then adapted it to his own historical framework [**doc. 30**].

Vergil completed the *Anglica Historia* in 1513, but it was only published, and then after considerable revision, in 1534. He rejected the annalistic tradition of the medieval chroniclers and divided English history into reigns. Those of the kings from Henry IV to Richard III possess, in his view, a unity of their own. They form a human drama directed by God, a period of vicious and destructive civil war. England is only delivered from this depressing period of her history by the accession of Henry VII. The origins of the conflict between the Houses of Lancaster and York lie in the usurpation of Henry IV. He broke his oath of allegiance to Richard II and deposed him. Though the 'good' king is exemplified by his son Henry V, Henry IV's sins were visited upon his grandson Henry VI. He was born to misery and deposed, amidst great bloodshed and disorder, by the House of York. Edward IV had broken his oath of allegiance and murdered Henry VI and later his own brother Clarence. Retribution was exacted in the fate of his sons, and the century reached a climax of evil and bloodshed in the usurpation and reign of Richard III (**38**, pp. 143–4). This framework was followed by Edward Hall in his influential work *The Union of the two Noble and Illustre families of Lancastre and Yorke* and finally the series of fifteenth-century plays by William Shakespeare. The sixteenth century possessed a fear of social revolt, foreign invasion and religious dissent which led writers to concentrate on the horrors and lessons of the Wars of the Roses. They sought reassurance and safety in an exalted respect for the monarchical authority of the Tudor dynasty.

Modern historians have largely rejected Vergil's framework for the fifteenth century. The origins of the wars clearly lie in the 1440s and 1450s, the majority reign of Henry VI. However, Vergil's portrait of internal disorder and social dislocation based on several contemporary sources is a different matter. An important aspect of the general misrule of Henry VI was the breakdown in law and order at a local level. This was made all the worse for the inhabitants because England was a country accustomed to relative peace and stability. There had been civil wars before in the middle ages, but at no stage had England been subjected to the ravaging and destruction that had befallen France during the Hundred Years War. Nor was England to experience anything like this in the Wars of the Roses. Nevertheless for a people accustomed to relative peace the breakdown in law and order in the middle decades of the fifteenth century was a worrying development. This concern was exacerbated by the fact that it was the recognised leaders of local society, the same men who were commissioned to keep the peace in the shires, who were leading their armed retainers around the countryside in pursuit of their personal feuds. The Commons voiced their concern on numerous occasions. In 1450 they declared that the realm was troubled by a wave of lawlessness which was greater than ever before; at the end of the decade they complained of robberies, riots and extortions (**28**, p. 9). The Paston letters describe vividly the raids and abuses of local justice experienced by a rising gentry family in East Anglia. Yet in comparison with the north, Wales and the south-west, East Anglia was relatively 'peaceful'. In general the level of violence in England during the Wars of the Roses was low compared to the continent but it was enough to turn public opinion decisively against Henry VI and his government.

The wars, then, originated from the misrule of Henry VI. However, what of the social and economic dislocation caused by the wars themselves? It has been calculated that there were at least sixty-one weeks of campaigning, and that there were major campaigns in ten out of the thirty years from 1455 to 1485 (**35**, p. 214). The social class most heavily involved was the nobility, but the wars did not result in the wholesale destruction of the 'old nobility'. The percentages of failures in the male line of peers for the last two quarters of the century were in fact below the average for the later middle ages (**48**, pp. 172–6). Nevertheless, many nobles perished in the wars, at least thirty-eight peers in battle or soon afterwards, during the period 1455–87 (**35**, p. 209). For the losers and their relatives there was the added threat of attainder and forfeiture. Between 1453 and

1504, 397 people, excluding members of the two principal royal houses, were attainted for treason. At least 256 had their attainders reversed, but years might have elapsed in the meantime (**44**, p. 129). Some lost everything, such as the Duke of Exeter who went into exile in 1461, where he was seen by Philippe de Commynes 'walking barefooted . . . begging his livelihood from house to house without revealing his identity' (**1**, p. 180). The participation of the nobles, which was at its highest in 1459–61 and 1470–1, was probably paralleled by that of the gentry, their immediate dependants in the intricate network of social and economic relationships existing in later medieval England (see pp. 9–12).

What of the lower classes in the towns and countryside? There were few actual urban sieges in the wars, but this did not preclude towns from taking measures to defend themselves. London and Coventry both possessed sufficiently strong defences to repel attacks in 1471. Moreover, since people and wealth were concentrated in the towns, they were an obvious source for the raising of troops and war finance. The evidence precludes any general conclusions, but the towns of Coventry, Norwich and Hull certainly seem to have contributed large sums in taxation for the war. York cannot have been alone in raising large contingents of men for military service on several occasions. Such exactions can only have disturbed the day-to-day life of these towns (**35**, pp. 219–20).

Many commoners were also involved in the wars. Their motives were usually a compound of national and local grievances. Some areas, notably Kent, seem to have acquired a reputation for rebellious tendencies. Many commoners were probably influenced by propaganda denouncing faction-ridden government and turned out for 'national heroes' like the Earl of Warwick. In the popular mind there was a firm connection between evil counsel given to the King and financial and judicial oppressions. If those oppressions brought political and military failure, then the lower classes could react violently, as they did in 1450. The breakdown of the natural social structure could also adversely affect the commoners. They expected the nobility and gentry to rule them and protect their interests as they had done in the past. In 1469 the Yorkshire rebellion of Robin of Holderness aimed at restoring the Percy family to the earldom of Northumberland and their traditional position of authority in the region. 'New men' often found it difficult to gain local trust. However, it is not easy to generalise about the various grievances and motives which stimulated the lower classes to often violent action (**35**, pp. 203–208).

Therefore it would seem that the wars affected many people from all classes, quite apart from the nobility and their adherents. The immediate consequences of battle may have been slight and relatively little soaked in blood, but the social and political instability was real enough. However, there was a determination on the part of the military commanders not to allow the campaigns to develop into the highly destructive '*chevauchées*' that characterised the Hundred Years War in France. Lords did not wish to destroy estates they coveted, but above all they did not want to alienate public opinion. Some depredation was inevitable, particularly if armies were unpaid or short of supplies, but in general there was a lack of pillaging and destruction. The one exception to the 'peacefulness' of armies was Margaret of Anjou's northern host of 1461. Significantly its activities stimulated opposition in the south, and particularly in London.

Richard III

> I am determined to prove a villain
> And hate the idle pleasures of these days.
>
> '*Richard III*' (Act 1 Scene 1), Shakespeare

One of the most controversial figures in English history is Richard III. His character and motives have exerted a compulsive fascination on historians and general writers alike. He has had savage critics and ardent admirers, though most historians tend to adopt a moderate approach to the last Plantagenet king of England. The instigator of this unending controversy was the Tudor playwright of genius, William Shakespeare.

In his famous play, Shakespeare presents Richard as the personification of arch-villainy. In Act 1 he is firmly identified as a conspiring fiend. His limp and hunchback are stressed, as is his withered arm in Act 3. The villainy is accentuated by the fact that he commits his evil deeds with an unbounded glee in his wickedness, untouched by any twinge of conscience. The only remorse comes late in the play, reaching a dramatic climax in Richard's ghost-ridden dreams on the eve of Bosworth.

The principal source for Shakespeare was, directly or indirectly, Edward Hall's *The Union of the two Noble and Illustre families of Lancastre and Yorke* (1548). In his attitude to Richard, Hall reflected the propaganda of the Tudor government, a staunch Protestantism and his own chauvinism. He portrayed Richard as a monster from whose evil rule England was delivered by a divine saviour in the shape of Henry VII. Hall was capable of deliberately twisting or suppressing historical facts to suit this basic framework. For the years 1483–5, he relied on Sir Thomas More for Richard's usurpation and mostly on Polydore Vergil for his reign, with some additions from the various London Chronicles.

This leads us to the 'twin architects' of the so-called 'Tudor Tradition' of Richard III – Polydore Vergil and Sir Thomas More (**56**, p. xxii). Vergil's *Anglica Historia* is the more important work of the two (see pp. 61–2). It covers the entire reign whereas More's *The History of King Richard III* ends abruptly on the eve of Buckingham's rebellion. Vergil's account has much more claim to be regarded as a sober and serious history. He was too conscientious a historian to suppress all the evidence of good rule carried out by Richard, though he attributes it to malicious designs [**doc. 26**]. Vergil completed the first draft of his work in 1513 and it seems likely that More used a manuscript as the basis for his *History* which was probably finished about 1520–1 (**37**, pp. 146–7). More's work has been interpreted in a number of ways but not as an essay in historical research. He set about the character of Richard with a decided relish, creating a villain 'entirely removed from the sphere of human life; he is evil incarnate, sheer monster' (**51**, p. 422). More was no historian; he was indulging himself by writing a clever literary piece in which the central character dramatically symbolised the tyranny which, according to his friend Erasmus, More loathed with an intense hatred (**56**, p. xxx).

It is wrong to view the works of Vergil and More as being primarily products of official Tudor propaganda. They were building upon an impression of Richard already accepted in their own time and for some years previously. Some of the contributions to this prevailing view were blatantly partisan, such as that of John Rous, the Warwickshire antiquary. His wish to attract patronage led him to give two diametrically opposed views of Richard III (see p. 57). The first, in the Rous Roll (which fortunately survived his attempts at destruction following the accession of Henry VII) was highly favourable. The second, in his *History of the Kings of England*, was distinctly unfavourable, portraying Richard as physically and spiritually deformed, the very Antichrist [**doc. 27**]. The portrait of Bernard André adds little to that of Rous 'Mark II'. However, as Henry VII's poet laureate and royal historiographer, André probably gives us the view that the first Tudor king wished to present of events leading to his success at Bosworth. Richard is a monster, delighting in his evil deeds, while Henry is the agent of divine retribution. Both André and probably Rous were writing for the King but there is very little evidence that Henry and his supporters took positive steps to blacken Richard's character (**37**, p. 191). To make matters worse for the modern defenders of Richard III, there is strong contemporary evidence that he provoked widespread mistrust and dislike. Whereas the alleged physical characteristics of Richard III do not stand up to close examination, the more sensible aspects of the Tudor Tradition would therefore appear to be supported by contemporary opinion.

The most important contemporary accounts for the reign of Richard III are the London Chronicles, Dominic Mancini's *The Usurpation of Richard III* and above all, the *Second Continuation of the Croyland Chronicle*. *The Great Chronicle* compiled by Robert Fabyan, is the most valuable of the London Chronicles. The section on Richard's reign was probably written around 1500, perhaps earlier, which was before the Tudor Tradition was firmly established. There is no mention of Richard's supposed physical deformities. However, of much greater importance is the record of fears and rumours that were circulating in London during Richard's protectorate and reign. The existence of this atmosphere of suspicion is confirmed by Mancini.

Dominic Mancini wrote his account of Richard's usurpation before 1 December 1483. It was written for his patron Angelo Cato, Archbishop of Vienne. Mancini was probably in England from the summer of 1482 until his recall in June of the following year, so he was very much in the right place at the right time. His account is sober and objective, avoiding the moralising and invented speeches so typical of many humanist works. Mancini believed that Richard intended to take the throne soon after the death of Edward IV, but he also shows that many other people thought the same in London in the spring of 1483 [**doc. 24**]. His importance is as a reporter of opinion, as his famous comment on the fate of the princes demonstrates. Mancini does not state, as later Tudor writers would do, that the princes had been murdered; he was in fact unable to discover their fate [**doc. 28**] (**56** p. xlii).

The most important single source for the reign is the *Croyland Chronicle*. The author was probably John Russell, Bishop of Lincoln. He was also a doctor of canon law, a royal councillor, Keeper of the Privy Seal to Edward IV (1474–83) and Chancellor to Richard (June 1483–July 1485), making him a remarkably well-informed author and one who wrote very soon after the events he describes.

He completed the work on the last day of April 1486. His view also commands great respect because, in the spirit of the Renaissance, he set out to be objective. The only exception to his objectivity was his marked prejudice against northerners. He is generally favourable to Edward IV but clearly disapproved of the usurpation and most of the reign of Richard III. This leads him to welcome Henry VII in the most glowing terms. In all likelihood Polydore Vergil had access to Russell's work. Thus Vergil's account of the reign of Richard III is based on a strictly contemporary source (**37**, pp. 135–142).

Mancini and Croyland are reliable sources, so where does that leave the character of Richard III? The succession of a Woodville-dominated king undoubtedly posed a threat to Richard's position, but whether it justified his usurpation is another matter. Contemporaries thought not. Richard's story of either Edward IV's bastardy or that of his sons was far too convenient and altogether unconvincing. He had attacked the laws of inheritance and was a usurper. The usurpation was carried out ruthlessly. All potential or actual opponents – Rivers, Grey, Vaughan, Hastings and finally the princes – were removed permanently. The fate of the two princes has been one of history's unending mysteries. This is rather surprising, since if, as seems likely, they were dead by autumn 1483, then the decision to kill them can only have been taken by Richard. He certainly had the best of motives and his experience of the Readeption of Henry VI showed the dangers of allowing rival claimants to live, even in the confines of the Tower. The most recently discovered evidence points an accusing finger at the Duke of Buckingham, though it largely depends on the interpretation of the word 'vise' which could be 'advice' or 'design' [**doc. 28**]. Yet it is inconceivable that a decision to murder the princes could have been taken without the knowledge and consent of Richard. Just as the ultimate responsibility for the deaths of Henry VI, Prince Edward and Clarence rests with Edward IV, so that of the princes lies with Richard. His opportunities and motives were sufficient to persuade contemporaries, who apparently believed the princes were dead in a matter of weeks after Richard's accession [**doc. 28**].

Richard was not without abilities. He was a genuinely pious and religious man, possibly due to the influence of his mother, Cecily of York, who was renowned for her piety. However, this did not stop him labelling her son Edward IV, or her grandsons, bastards. Richard also publicly expressed a concern for sexual morality, but this was in large part just a device for smearing the reputations of his enemies, such as the Woodvilles and the supporters of Henry Tudor. Yet Richard himself was not altogether innocent, for he had two bastards, a son and a daughter.

Many defenders of Richard III have drawn attention to the fact that he proved an energetic and efficient ruler. He moved continually around the kingdom, partly in the interests of defence but also to show himself to his subjects and supervise local administration. However, it is his Parliament which has provoked greatest admiration. The most important legislation was designed to remove some of the shortcomings of the legal system. A partially effective attempt was made to tighten up property rights. A suspected felon was given entitlement to bail and his goods were not to be seized before conviction. The qualifications for jury service in the shrieval courts were also made more stringent. Finally benevolences* were declared illegal. No-one can doubt the business acumen of the King and his ministers, but the legislation was primarily conceived as a bid for public confidence.

However, Richard was never able to win the general support of his kingdom. He never seems to have really overcome the widespread mistrust and suspicion generated by his usurpation and the disappearance of the princes. The Tudor Tradition was essentially a southern phenomenon, originating from contemporary opinion in southern England where Richard's rule seems to have been regarded as tyranny (see pp. 48–9). Yet what was tyranny in the south was 'good governance' in the north. The Council at York regarded Richard's death at Bosworth as a disaster, but its relationship to the King was essentially that of client and patron [**doc. 29**]. Richard remitted the city's taxes and upheld and extended its privileges; in return he expected and received military support. However, was an oligarchy of wealthy merchants representative of the north as a whole, or even of York? It is now impossible to know, but there are fragments of evidence suggesting that the commons of York did not accord Richard unanimous praise. The key to the general relationship between Richard and the north is probably the same as that with the Council of York – patron and client. Northern society benefited from his rule but quickly adapted to the new circumstances after 1485. It was of course two northern families who determined the issue on 22 August 1485.

13 Yorkist Government

After his victory at Tewkesbury in 1471, Edward IV could afford to be lenient to former Lancastrians. Among those who returned to England was Sir John Fortescue, former Chief Justice of the King's Bench and Chancellor to Henry VI. Before his death in 1479, Fortescue completed his famous treatise, *The Governance of England.* He attributed the problems of contemporary government to two basic causes: the insolvency of the crown and the overweening influence of the nobility. Fortescue did not look for a remedy in a more absolutist form of government such as that of Louis XI in France. He would have preferred to see the English monarchy strengthened within the existing constitutional framework, where the king ruled according to laws accepted by Parliament. This was to be achieved by traditionally prescribed methods to improve the royal finances and by the appointment of a more effective Council (**40**, pp. 490–2).

The Yorkist kings pursued a very similar course of action. They were not directly influenced by Fortescue but common sense and experience suggested it. Edward IV was a curious compound of hedonistic debauchery and administrative ability. He applied himself closely to business and was surrounded by very able and experienced councillors [**doc. 16**]. This application to governmental activities was certainly matched by Richard III. However, neither of them could quite parallel the energy and efficiency of Henry VII.

Edward's approach to the tasks of medieval kingship was essentially pragmatic. He recognised the need to strengthen the monarchy and thus maintain his own personal power. With this aim in mind, he utilised any means available to him, though in general 'he thought more in terms of new men rather than new institutions, or even the reform of old ones' (**54**, p. 301). Yorkist government was a highly personal system centred on the figure of the king. Both Edward and Richard bent their energies to making their wills felt in the kingdom and to demonstrating their concern for the welfare of their subjects. The clearest illustration of this new efficiency and personal control in government was the increased use of letters and warrants issued under the signet, the seal kept by the king's secretary. The signet was therefore a highly personal manifestation of the sovereign's authority. In the Yorkist period it was employed more frequently and in matters of greater importance than hitherto, being used to authorise royal grants, issue royal letters and administer the royal revenues. The activity of the signet was the principal reason for the increased importance of the king's secretary, paving the way for the great development under the Tudors.

English medieval kings always claimed the right to select their own advisers. However, the Lancastrians had often been forced to include leading nobles. The Yorkists were able to reverse this trend and increasingly summon whom they preferred, though in the 1460s there was always a Neville interest in the Council. Edward otherwise relied mostly on men who lacked baronial or ecclesiastical position but in return for his patronage rendered loyal and able service. Many were from a gentry background or were professional lawyers and administrators. The importance of this new secular ruling élite reflected both the highly personal nature of the reign and the limited support the Yorkists commanded amongst the established nobility. They staffed Edward's household, implementing his decisions, and were his principal advisers in the Council.

The Yorkist period witnessed a revival in the traditional administrative and judicial powers of the Council. It helped the king to formulate policy and relieved him of some of the day-to-day decisions of government. The revival of the Council merely reflected the energy and efficiency of Edward IV and his ministers. Richard III continued in a similar vein, largely relying on his faithful northerners after the rebellion of 1483. Edward's dependence on his 'new men' was in no sense innovatory. In the early twelfth century Henry I had pursued a similar policy. The importance of these men did not detract from the power of the nobility in Yorkist England. In no sense could the kings afford to ignore their greatest subjects. The nobles were always summoned to the Great Council when major topics were under consideration, such as war or foreign policy. However, their essential role was to uphold royal authority and law and order in their own localities. This obviously precluded any drastic reduction in noble power and it is in their attitude towards the nobles that the contrasts are most apparent between the Yorkist kings and Henry VII.

It is now clear that neither Edward IV nor Richard III took effective action to diminish the power of the nobility. In the crucial relationship with the nobles, the medieval monarchy possessed the great advantage of royal patronage in the form of titles, lands and offices. Edward IV proved very generous in the distribution of patronage during his first reign (see pp. 30–1). After the salutary experience of the Readeption he was more sparing in his distribution of titles and honours, limiting them largely to the royal family. Richard III was also sparing in his creations, though Lord Howard was made Duke of Norfolk and his son Earl of Surrey. However, he was lavish in his distribution of forfeited lands, principally to his northerners but also amongst the nobility (see pp. 48–50). Therefore it is difficult to conclude that the much-vaunted Yorkist proclamations and legislation against the abuses of livery and maintenance amounted to anything significant. Since they had placed local authority in the hands of 'overmighty' subjects, the Yorkists had to maintain their power.

The revival in the royal finances was the essential basis for the reassertion of monarchical authority in the late fifteenth century. Whereas Henry VI's government was in debt to the tune of about £372,000 by 1450, Edward IV died solvent in 1483. How did he achieve this remarkable turn-about? In 1467 Edward pledged himself in Parliament to 'live of his own'. He promised not to resort to parliamentary taxation, except for 'great and urgent causes' which concerned the defence and welfare of the realm [**doc. 31**]. In fact Parliament did vote the King £93,000 in the first reign, but the bulk of it was spent on such 'causes' as repressing rebellions and defensive requirements (**54**, p. 371).Edward would not therefore have been able, even had he wished, to follow the example of the Valois kings of France and solve the financial problems of the crown by taxing his subjects.

Edward IV was confronted by regular royal expenditure of some £50,000 per annum. This involved the costs of the royal households, provision for the royal family, governmental expenditure and a variety of military needs. To meet these demands, Edward had two principal sources of revenue: customs duties and the crown lands. The former were adversely affected by the trade depression and brought in only £25,000 on average per year until the trade improvement of the 1470s. The crown lands, swollen by the incorporation of the Yorkist estates, the forfeitures of 1461 and the series of acts of Resumption,* seemed to offer much greater potential (**54**, pp. 372–3).

Any examination of Yorkist finance centres upon the administration of the crown lands (**59**, pp. 51–65). This involved subjecting the bulk of the lands held by the king, whether by inheritance, forfeiture or wardship,* to the normal methods of contemporary estate management. They were put into groups, each under the control of specially-appointed professional receivers and surveyors. The origins of the system lay in the administration of the lands of the duchy of York, as the majority of the Lancastrian royal lands had been farmed out through the Exchequer. The latter, far too inefficient, was now by-passed and the estate officials were made to account to the chamber in the royal household. The revenues were thus immediately available to the monarch. This coincided with the rise of the chamber as both a revenue-collecting and spending department. Long before the end of Edward's reign it had superseded the Exchequer as the leading financial office of state.

The chamber system of finance was not new, but its efficient application gave the king a more direct personal control over his finances. However, it does not seem that the Yorkists achieved anything approaching the level of efficiency reached under Henry VII. Edward was primarily concerned with maintaining himself in power. He largely redistributed lands acquired in 1461 as patronage to reward his supporters and attract new ones. His acts of Resumption always included lists of exemptions. It was only in the second reign that Edward showed a consistent determination to accumulate and retain royal lands. However, there still seems to have remained 'a gap between theory and practice in estate management' (**54**, p. 383). Richard III appears to have appreciated this. A 'remembrance' survives from his reign proposing improvements in royal financial methods. As a great Marcher lord, Richard appreciated what his brother had begun, and he extended and improved it. He was concerned not to dissipate the crown lands, to which he had brought his extensive northern estates. Richard's lavish patronage was largely drawn from the extensive forfeitures of 1483. Nevertheless he did find himself in financial difficulties by 1485.

Edward IV developed other means of raising money. He resorted to various arbitrary methods such as the recoinage of 1464–5 and the notorious benevolences.* Edward was also very alive to the wealth of the merchant communities. He took a keen and direct interest in their activities and promoted trade through a series of commercial treaties. The merchants responded by extending him generous credit, as did foreign bankers. Edward's customs revenue also rose to an annual average of some £34,000 in the second reign. This was an important factor in the solvency of Edward's last years, but above all there was the annual French pension of 50,000 gold crowns from the Treaty of Picquigny (1475). In these last years the King was able 'to live of his own' [**doc. 32**]. His regular income has been calculated at some £60–70,000 in this period but this may be compared with the income of over £100,000 which Henry VII enjoyed at the end of his reign. However, 'the best testimony to the quality of Edward's financial policies is the degree to which the shrewd and calculating Henry held firm to them' (**54**, pp. 385–7). He was the first king of England to die solvent since the twelfth century.

The preservation of law and order was one of the most intractable problems of later medieval government. This was scarcely surprising in a society where there was no police force or standing army and most men carried weapons. The level of crime fluctuated during the fifteenth century and Yorkist England did witness an improvement on the dark and violent days of Henry VI. The first reign of Edward IV was not without its problems with the series of Lancastrian and Neville-inspired uprisings, local feuds and outbreaks of crime. Edward tackled this wave of disorder by using the existing legal system, but infusing it with a new efficiency through his own involvement and that of professional officials. He largely relied on the court of chivalry, commissions of oyer and terminer and his own activities. Edward travelled with a number of commissions and was always in court when he was keen to have a verdict of 'guilty' returned against the accused (**28**, p. 12). However, the real improvement in law and order came only after the Readeption. By the end of the Yorkist period, there was less despair about lawlessness, even if there was still a high level of crime, with some areas notorious for disorder. There had been a general improvement in the north but not in regions like Wales and the Marches. The 'Achilles heel' of Yorkist attempts to improve law and order was the kings' reluctance to make any serious attack on the system of livery and maintenance. Local government and justice remained firmly in the grip of noble patrons.

The accession of Richard III led to the most significant institutional development of Yorkist government. In Wales Edward had replaced Herbert rule with that of a council under the nominal leadership of the Prince of Wales supported by the Woodvilles and experienced professional administrators. Richard followed suit in his own region by creating the Council of the North, under an 'outsider', the Earl of Lincoln. He was aided by the leading northern families, including the Percies, though the Earl of Northumberland probably felt some resentment at Lincoln's position. The Council's functions were defined by a set of 'Regulations' issued in July 1484. It was vested with all powers of administration and justice in the region. Royal authority was thus brought directly into the north, in a manner followed by the later Tudors (**52**; **29**; **56**, pp. 181–3).

14 'The Wars of the Roses' up to Stoke

The battle of Bosworth settled the question of who was to be king of England. Richard III had lost the day, the kingdom and his life. His body was stripped naked, slung over the back of a horse and taken to Leicester for an undignified burial [**doc. 26**]. The victorious army acclaimed the new king with shouts of 'God save King Henry'. The crown which Richard had worn into battle was found on the field and placed upon Henry's head by Lord Stanley. Henry's hereditary title to the throne was rather weak, but that fact was irrelevant in the summer of 1485. The god of war had strikingly confirmed Henry's claim to the kingdom

Henry VII was crowned with splendid ceremony in Westminster Abbey in October 1485. His title to the throne was accepted in the Parliament of the following month. Both the lords and the Commons then urged the King to fulfil his promise, made in exile, of marrying Edward IV's daughter, Elizabeth of York. After gaining the necessary papal dispensation, Henry and Elizabeth were married in January 1486. The families of Lancaster and York were thus united but the fighting was not over.

Henry faced a series of challenges to his throne, but he responded rapidly and decisively to all the threats. It was an age of pretenders, reflecting the lack of any feasible alternative candidates to the first Tudor king. The most serious rebellion came in 1487. Lambert Simnel first claimed to be Edward IV's younger son Richard, Duke of York, and then quickly changed his identity to the Earl of Warwick, the son of Clarence. Warwick was in fact firmly under Henry's control in the Tower. Simnel's backers attracted the support of Richard III's nephew and acknowledged heir, the Earl of Lincoln, but the movement lacked any real support in England. The issue was settled in Henry's favour at the hard-fought battle of Stoke in June 1487. The Tudor dynasty was now firmly established.

There were intermittent threats to Henry VII in the last decade of the century, principally from another pretender Perkin Warbeck, but his throne was never in any real danger. Peace and stability gradually returned to England and Henry was able to continue the reconstruction of monarchical power begun by Edward IV. Many of the latter's servants and officials had supported Tudor in 1485 and now staffed Henry's government and court. Certainly in political and administrative terms, the reign of Henry VII represented the continuity of York after the savage but brief interlude of Richard III's reign. Henry completed the recovery of the crown and the kingdom from the wars of Lancaster and York, a recovery which had been jeopardised by the personal ambitions of the Earl of Warwick and Richard, Duke of Gloucester. By the time he died in 1509 he had set the stage for the political, social and cultural achievements of the Tudor monarchy in the sixteenth century.

Part Four: Documents

The historian of the fifteenth century is not particularly well-served by contemporary written sources. The great series of monastic chronicles which depict so vividly the political and social events in previous centuries, comes to an end in 1422 with the death of Thomas Walsingham of St Albans. Nevertheless the situation is nowhere near as bad as one literary expert, William Nicolson, believed at the end of the seventeenth century. He commented that historians were so bewildered by the shortcomings of the source material that they were unable 'to form a regular History out of such a vast Heap of Rubbish and Confusion' (**42**, p. 229).

The national and local chronicles which serve the middle decades of the fifteenth century are sufficient to reconstruct the political and military events of the period, but they incorporate only limited insight and all too often contain long and rather tedious accounts of ceremonies and pageants. With very rare exceptions, the mentalities of the principal characters in the Wars of the Roses may be gauged only from their actions. There is no disguising the fact that fifteenth-century historians sorely lack the state papers and personal correspondence which so graphically bring to life the motives and inner thoughts of statesmen in the Tudor period. Admittedly, there are several collections of correspondence surviving from the fifteenth century, the most famous being the letters of the Paston family. However, it is now clear that the experiences of the family in East Anglia were by no means typical of the English gentry as a whole (see p. 11).

Another problem for the fifteenth-century historian is the peculiar difficulties associated with works written during or shortly after periods of civil war. Such accounts are almost inevitably distorted by partisan considerations and private fears or aspirations. This of course is very much the case with the source material for the Wars of the Roses. Much of this book has been concerned with evaluating the reliability of works like that of John Blacman (see pp. 52–4) for the character of Henry VI and those of John Rous (see p. 66) and Polydore Vergil (see pp. 66–8) for the activities of

Richard III, and indeed everything associated with the so-called 'Tudor Tradition'.

Fortunately the end of the period is better served by written sources. With the Italians – Dominic Mancini (see p. 67) and Polydore Vergil – the historian encounters a new world of sophisticated observation of contemporary events. To their important works may be added the valuable *Second Continuation of the Croyland Chronicle* (see pp. 67–8) which provides the best general account of the reign of Edward IV, particularly for the last thirteen years, and also of that of Richard III.

The extracts which follow are drawn from many of the major sources for the Wars of the Roses, including all of those mentioned above. Within the space available only a small selection has been possible. They have been selected for three reasons: first they present some of the themes and characters discussed in this book; second, they show the nature of society during the wars; and finally, they illustrate some of the problems associated with fifteenth-century sources.

Spelling and punctuation have been modernised for ease of reading.

document 1

Bolingbroke's claim to the crown, 30 September 1399

In the name of Father, Son and Holy Ghost, I, Henry of Lancaster, challenge this realm of England and the crown with all the members and the appurtenances, as I that am descended by right line of the blood coming from the good Lord Henry third, and through that right that God of his grace hath sent me with help of my kin and of my friends to recover it, the which realm was in point to be undone for default of governance and undoing of the good laws.

From *Rotuli Parliamentorum*, vol. 3, pp. 422–3.

document 2

The Congress of Arras, August–September 1435

. . . the parties gathered at the place of conference for several days, and the delegations drafted several treaties and put them forward, but these were very difficult and different from one another. Those who represented King Charles insisted that the King of England must stop and desist from calling himself King of France any more, conceding that on certain conditions he would be granted the duchies of Guienne and Normandy; but those who represented King Henry would not agree to this at all, so they parted ill contented, and went away to their lodgings.

So on 5th September, after taking leave of the Duke and Duchess of Burgundy, the Cardinal of Winchester led the entire English delegation out of Arras without having reached any agreement with the French. . . . And they suspected what in fact was to happen soon afterwards, that is to say that King Charles and the Duke of Burgundy were growing cordial towards each other. For they perceived even before their departure that those two parties had a great liking for one another. . . . Soon after the departure of the English ambassadors from the town of Arras. . . . the French and the Burgundians met together in conference at the accustomed place, where they had a great discussion together about various matters . . . and they agreed to make a final peace between King Charles on the one hand and Duke Philip of Burgundy on the other.

From Jean de Waurin *Recueil des Croniques* (**24**), vol. 4, pp. 69–87; also *English Historical Documents* (**16**), pp. 252–3.

document 3

Henry VI's Cession of Maine, 22 December 1445

To the most high and powerful prince, our very dear uncle of France (Charles VII) . . .

Most high and powerful prince, our very dear uncle, knowing that you would be very glad that we should make deliverance of the city, town and castle of Le Mans, and of all that we have and hold within the comté of Maine, to the most high and powerful prince and our very dear father and uncle, the king of Sicily and Charles of Anjou, his brother (as by your subjects and ambassadors at this time sent to us has been more fully said and explained), who have most affectionately upon your part required us so to do, and moreover informed us that it appeared to you that this was one of the best and aptest means to arrive at the blessing of a peace between us and you; wishing effectually to prove the great desire and affection which we have to attain unto the said blessing of peace, . . . favouring also our most dear and well-beloved companion the queen, who has requested us to do this many times . .

Dated at Windsor, the xxij. day of December, in the year one thousand cccc. and forty-five.

Thus signed, HENRY.

From Stevenson (**21**), vol. II part 2, pp. 639–642.

document 4

John Blacman's Description of King Henry VI

He was, like a second Job, a man simple and upright, altogether fearing the Lord God, and departing from evil. He was a simple man, without any crook of craft or untruth . . .

He was both upright and just, always keeping to the straight line of justice in his acts. Upon none would he wittingly inflict any injustice. To God and the Almighty he rendered most faithfully that which was His, for he took pains to pay in full the tithes and offerings due to God and the Church: and this he accompanied with sedulous devotion . . .

A diligent and sincere worshipper of God was this king, more given to God and to devout prayer than to handling worldly and temporal things, or practising vain sports and pursuits: these he despised as trifling, and was continually occupied either in prayer or the reading of the scriptures or of chronicles . . .

This King Henry was chaste and pure from the beginning of his days. He eschewed all licentiousness in word or deed while he was young; until he was of marriageable age, when he espoused the most noble lady, Lady Margaret, daughter of the King of Sicily, by whom he begat one only son, the most noble and virtuous Prince Edward; and with her and toward her he kept his marriage vow wholly and sincerely . . .

It happened once, that at Christmas time a certain great lord brought before him a dance or show of young ladies with bared bosoms who were to dance in that guise before the king . . . but the king was not blind to it, nor unaware of the devilish wile, and spurned the delusion, and very angrily averted his eyes, turned his back upon them, and went out to his chamber, saying: 'Fy, Fy, for shame, forsother ye be to blame'.

Besides, he took great precautions to secure not only his own chastity but that of his servants. For before he was married, being as a youth a pupil of chastity, he would keep careful watch through hidden windows of his chamber, lest any foolish impertinence of women . . . cause the fall of any of his household.

John Blacman (**12**), pp. 4–14.

document 5

Treasonable Language against Henry VI, 1450

It is to be inquired for our sovereign lord the king whether John Merfeld of Brightling in the shire of Sussex, husbandman, and William Merfeld of Brightling in the shire aforesaid, husbandman, at Brightling in the open market the Sunday in the feast of St Anne, the 28th year of our sovereign lord (26 July 1450), falsely said that the king was a natural fool and would often hold a staff in his hands with a bird on the end, playing therewith as a fool, and that another king must be ordained to rule the land, saying that the king was no person able to rule the land.

[An endorsement shows that on 1 July 1451 a grand jury declared this to be a true bill.]

English Historical Documents (**16**), p. 264.

document 6

A Contrast between the rule of Henry V and that of Henry VI, c.1455

The Praise of Henry V

O good lord God, why did you let so soon to pass
This noble prince, that in all Christianity
Had then no peer in any land, no more nor less;
So excellent was his happy truth
In flourishing age of all freshness of youth
That might have let him live to greater age
Till he had wholly gained his heritage.

Above all things, he kept the law and peace
Throughout all England, that no insurrection
Nor any riots were not made to cease.
No neighbours' war remained without correction

But peaceably all under his protection
Complaints of wrongs always in general
Reformed were under his justice equal.

The Exhortation to Henry VI

In every shire with jacks and salets clean
Misrule does rise, and makes the neighbours war.
The weaker goes beneath, as oft is seen,
The mightiest his quarrel will prefer
That poor men's causes are set back too far,
Which if the peace and law were well conserved
Might be amended, and thanks of God deserved.

They kill your men always by one and one.
And he who shall say aught shall be crushed doubtless;
For in your realm is no just peace; there are none
That dare aught now the quarrellers suppress.
Such sickness now hath taken them and excess,
They will naught heed of riot or debate,
So common is it now in each state.

(trans. *English Historical Documents* (**16**), pp. 274–5).

Withstand, good lord, the outbreak of debates,
And chastise well also the rioters
Who in each shire are now confederates
Against your peace, and all their maintainers;
For truly else will fall the fairest flowers
Of your great crown and noble monarchy,
Which God defend and keep through his mercy.

Who prays to you for any countenance,
Whether he be Duke, Earl, or other estate,
Blame him for the very maintenance
Of such misrule, contact and all debate:
Which else your law would chastise and abate,
If maintainers would allow it to have the course
That plaintiffs might to law have their recourse.

John Hardyng (**8**), pp. 744–9.

document 7

The death of William de la Pole, Duke of Suffolk, April 1450

As on Monday next after May Day [4 May] there came tidings to London, that on Thursday before the Duke of Suffolk came unto the coasts of Kent very near Dover with his two ships and a little pinnace; the which pinnace he sent with certain letters to certain of his trusted men towards Calais, to know how he would be received; and with him met a ship called the *Nicholas of the Tower*, with other ships waiting on him, and from those who were in the pinnace the master of the *Nicholas* had knowledge of the duke's coming. And when he espied the duke's ships, he sent forth his boat to know what they were, and the duke himself spoke to them and said that he was by the king's commandment sent to Calais. And they said he must speak with their master; and so he with two or three of his men went forth with them in their boat to the *Nicholas*. And when he came, the master bade him 'Welcome traitor!' as men say; and after this the master desired to know if the shipmen wished to support the duke, and they sent word that they would not in any way; and so he was in the *Nicholas* until the following Saturday.

Some say he wrote many thanks to be delivered to the king, but that is not truly known. He had his confessor with him. And some say that he was arraigned in the ship, in their way, upon the impeachments, and found guilty.

. . . And in the sight of all men he was drawn out of the great ship into the boat, and there was an axe and a block; and one of the most ignorant of the ship bade him lay down his head, and he should be fairly treated, and die by a sword; and the man took a rusty sword, and smote off his head with half a dozen strokes, and took away his gown of russet, and his doublet of velvet sewn with metal rings, and laid his body on the sands of Dover.

Extract from a letter of William Lomnor to John Paston, 5 May 1450. *The Paston Letters* (**17**), vol. 1, p. 124. Also *English Historical Documents* (**16**), pp. 263–4.

document 8

Cade's Rebellion, May 1450

And this same year, in the month of May, arose the men of Kent and made themselves a captain, a ribald, an Irishman, called John

Cade, who at the beginning took upon him the name of a gentleman and called himself Mortimer for to have the favour of the people. And he called himself John Amend-All, for as much as then and long before the realm of England had been ruled by untrue counsel, wherefore the common profit was sore hurt and deceased; so that the common people, what with taxes and tallages and other oppressions, might not live by their handiwork and husbandry, wherefore they grudged sore against those who had the governance of the land.

An English Chronicle (**2**), pp. 64–5.

document 9

Thomas Yonge's Plea in Parliament, May 1451

In the same parliament Thomas Yonge of Bristol, apprentice in law, moved that because the king had no offspring, it would be for the security of the kingdom that it should be openly known who should be heir apparent. And he named the duke of York. For which cause the same Thomas was afterwards committed to the Tower of London.

Annales rerum anglicarum from (**21**), vol. II, part 2, p. 770. It has now been conclusively shown that the 'Annales' were not written – as earlier assumed – by the antiquary, William Worcester.

document 10

York made Protector, 27 March 1454

. . . the said duke shall be chief of the king's council, and devised therefore for the said duke a name different from other councillors, not the name of tutor, lieutenant, governor, nor of regent, nor no name that shall import authority of government of the land; but the said name of protector and defender, the which importeth a personal duty of intendence to the actual defence of this land, as well against th'enemies outward, if case require, as against rebels inward, if any hap to be, that God forbid, during the king's pleasure, and so that it be not prejudice to my Lord Prince . . .

From *Rotuli Parliamentorum*, vol. 5, p. 242.

document 11

Henry VI regains his sanity, Christmas 1454.

. . . Blessed be God, the King is well amended, and hath been since Christmas day, and on St John's day commanded his almoner to ride to Canterbury with his offering, and commanded his secretary to offer at St Edward's.

And on Monday afternoon the Queen came to him, and brought my lord Prince with her. And then he asked what the Prince's name was, and the Queen told him Edward; and then he held up his hands and thanked God thereof. And he said he never knew till that time, nor wist not what was said to him, nor wist not where he had been whilst he hath been sick till now.

Extract from a letter of Edmund Clere to John Paston, 9 January 1455. *The Paston Letters* (**17**), vol. 1, p. 345.

document 12

The Rule of Henry VI and Margaret of Anjou

In this same time, the realm of England was out of all good governance, as it had been many days before, for the king was simple and led by covetous counsel, and owed more than he was worth. His debts increased daily, but payment was there none; all the possessions and lordships that pertained to the crown the king had given away, some to lords and some to other lesser persons, so that he had almost nothing left to own. And such impositions as were put to the people, as taxes and tallages, all that came from them was spent in vain, for he held no household nor maintained any wars. For these misgovernances, and for many other, the hearts of the people were turned away from them that had the governance of the land, and their blessings were turned into cursing.

The queen with such as were of her affinity ruled the realm as she liked, gathering innumerable riches. . . . The queen was defamed and slandered, that he that was called Prince, was not her son, but a bastard gotten in adultery; wherefore she dreading that he should not succeed his father as king of England, allied unto her all the knights and squires of Cheshire for to have their benevolence, and held open household among them; and made her son called the Prince give a livery of Swans to all the gentlemen of the county, and to many other throughout the land; trusting through their strength to make her son king . . .

An English Chronicle (**2**), pp. 79–80.

document 13

The Attainder of the Yorkist Leaders at Coventry, November 1459

Wherefore please it your highness, these premises considered, by the advice and assent of your lords spiritual and temporal and of your commons assembled in this your parliament, and by the authority of the same to ordain, establish and enact, that the said . . . Richard Duke of York, Edward Earl of March, Richard Earl of Salisbury, Edmund Earl of Rutland, Richard Earl of Warwick . . . for their said traitorous levying of war against your said most noble person, at Ludford . . . be declared attainted of high treason, as false traitors and enemies against your most noble person, high majesty, crown, and dignity. . . . And that they and every one of them, forfeit from them and their heirs, by the same authority, all their estates, honours and dignities, which they or any of them have within this your realm of England, and within Wales and Ireland.

From *Rotuli Parliamentorum*, vol. 5, p. 349.

document 14

The Act of Accord, 24 October 1460

20. . . . the said Richard Duke of York, tenderly desiring the weal, peace and prosperity of this land, and to set apart all that might be trouble to the same; and considering the possession of the said King Henry the Sixth, and that he hath . . . been named, taken and reputed King of England and of France, with the royal estate, dignity and preeminence belonging thereto, and Lord of Ireland, during his life natural; . . . the said Duke without hurt or prejudice of his [own] said right and title, shall take, worship and honour him [Henry] for his sovereign lord.

22. Item, it is accorded, appointed and agreed, that the said Richard Duke of York be entitled, called and reputed from henceforth, very and rightful heir to the Crowns, Royal Estate, Dignity and Lordship abovesaid; and after the death of the said

Henry . . . the said Duke and his heirs, shall immediately succeed to the said Crowns, Royal Estate, Dignity and Lordship.

23. Item, the said Richard Duke of York, shall have by authority of the present Parliament, Castles, Manors, Lands and Tenements, with the Wards, Marriages, Reliefs, Services, Fines, Amercements, Offices, Advowsons, Fees, and other appurtenances to them belonging, whatsoever they be, to the yearly value of 10,000 marks, over all charges and reprises: whereof 5,000 marks shall be to his own estate, 3,500 marks to Edward, his first son, earl of March, for his estate, and £1,000 to Edmund, Earl of Rutland, his second son, for his yearly sustentation; for such considerations, and to such intent, as shall be declared by the Lords of the King's Council.

From *Rotuli Parliamentorum*, vol. 5, pp. 378–9.

document 15

An Indenture between Richard Neville, Earl of Warwick, and Sir John Trafford, 1461

This indenture made the 26 day of May the first year of the reign of the king our sovereign lord Edward IV between Richard Neville, Earl of Warwick and Captain of Calais, on the one hand, and Sir John Trafford, who of his free and mere motion is pledged and retained towards and with the earl during the term of his life, to be with him and do him service and attendance against all manner of persons, saving his allegiance. And that Sir John Trafford shall be ready at the desire or commandment of the earl to come unto him at all such times and in such places as the earl shall call upon him or give him sufficient warning, horsed, harnessed, arrayed, and accompanied as the case shall require, and according to what the earl shall call him to do, at the reasonable costs of the said earl. And the earl for the same has granted to Sir John Trafford to have by patent under the seal of his arms in annuity during his life of the sum of 20 marks sterling to be levied, taken, and received of the issues and revenues of his lordship of Middleham by the hands of his receiver there at the times of Michaelmas and Easter . . .

English Historical Documents (**16**), p. 1126.

document 16

The Character of Edward IV

Edward was of a gentle nature and cheerful aspect: nevertheless should he assume an angry countenance he could appear very terrible to beholders. He was easy of access to his friends and others, even the least notable. Frequently he called to his side complete strangers, when he thought that they had come with the intention of addressing or beholding him more closely. He was wont to show himself to those who wished to watch him, and he seized any opportunity that the occasion offered of revealing his fine stature more protractedly and more evidently to on-lookers. He was so genial in his greeting, that if he saw a newcomer bewildered at his appearance and royal magnificence, he would give him courage to speak by laying a kindly hand upon his shoulder. To plaintiffs and to those who complained of injustice he lent a willing ear; charges against himself he contented with an excuse if he did not remove the cause. He was more favourable than other princes to foreigners, who visited his realm for trade or for any other reason. He very seldom showed munificence, and then only in moderation, still he was very grateful to those from whom he had received a favour. Though not rapacious of other men's goods, he was yet so eager for money, that in pursuing it he acquired a reputation for avarice. He adopted this artifice for piling up wealth: when an assembly from the whole kingdom was convened, he would set forth how he had incurred many expenses, and must unavoidably prepare for much further expenditure by land and sea for the defence of the realm. It was just, he said, that these sums should be repaid by the public in whose benefit they were spent.

Thus, by appealing to causes, either true or at least with some semblance of truth, he did not appear to extort but almost to beg for subsidies. He behaved similarly with private individuals, but with them at times more imperiously: and so he had gathered great treasures, whose size had not made him more generous or prompt in disbursement than when he was poor, but rather much more stringent and tardy, so that now his avarice was publicly proclaimed. For the same reason he is believed to have abandoned the Flemings, for, had he given them succour against Louis the king of France, he would have ceased to receive from Louis fifty thousand scuts [crowns] each year. He knew that he would receive them just as long as he refrained from assisting the Flemings.

In food and drink he was most immoderate: it was his habit, so I have learned, to take an emetic for the delight of gorging his stomach once more. For this reason and for the ease, which was especially dear to him after his recovery of the crown, he had grown fat in the loins, whereas previously he had been not only tall but rather lean and very active. He was licentious in the extreme: moreover it was said that he had been most insolent to numerous women after he had seduced them, for, as soon as he grew weary of dalliance, he gave up the ladies much against their will to the other courtiers. He pursued with no discrimination the married and unmarried, the noble and lowly: however he took none by force. He overcame all by money and promises, and having conquered them, he dismissed them.

Dominic Mancini (**14**), pp. 64–67.

document 17

The Marriage of Edward IV, 1 May 1464

Also the fourth year of King Edward, the Earl of Warwick was sent into France for a marriage for the King. . . . And while the said Earl of Warwick was in France, the king was wedded to Elizabeth Gray, widow, the which Sir John Gray that was her husband was slain at York field [Towton] in King Harry's party; and the same Elizabeth was daughter to the Lord Rivers; and the wedding was privily in a secret place, the first day of May, the year above said. And when the Earl of Warwick came home and heard this, then he was greatly displeased with the king; and after that great dissension rose ever more and more between the king and him, for that and other causes.

John Warkworth (**23**), p. 3.

document 18

The Feud between Henry, Lord Grey of Codnor, and Henry Vernon, 1467–8

In the month of November a horrible murder was committed in a certain part near Derby, when the man of Lord Grey of Codnor killed [a man in the service of Henry]* Vernon, esquire. For this reason and for others, the lord King set up a commission of oyer and terminer in the county of Derby [3 January 1468]. Around the king they favoured Lord Grey; and the Duke of Clarence favoured the Lord Earl of Shrewsbury and Vernon.

* A blank in the manuscript.

Annales rerum anglicarum from (**21**), vol. II, part 2, pp. 788–9.

document 19

The Alliance between Margaret of Anjou and the Earl of Warwick, July 1470

Sforza de Bettini of Florence, Milanese Ambassador in France, to Galeazzo Maria Sforza, Duke of Milan.

Angers, 24 July 1470.
The Queen of England and the Prince of Wales, her son, arrived here the day before yesterday, and on the same day the Earl of Warwick also arrived. The same evening the king presented him to the queen. With great reverence Warwick went on his knees and asked her pardon for the injuries and wrongs done to her in the past. She graciously forgave him and he afterwards did homage and fealty there, swearing to be a faithful and loyal subject of the king, queen, and prince as his liege lords unto his death . . .

Angers, 28 July 1470.
The marriage of Warwick's daughter to the Prince of Wales is settled and announced. His Majesty has sent for the lady to Amboise, where the marriage will be consummated. In two days Warwick will leave for his fleet.

From *Calendar of State Papers and Manuscripts, Milan*, ed. A. B. Hinds (London, 1913) vol. 1, p. 138.

document 20

A Letter from the Earl of Warwick to Louis XI, 13 February 1471

Sir, I commend myself to your good grace in the humblest possible way. And may it please you to know that I have received your letters by this messenger, by which I have learnt that now war has begun between you, your adversary, and ours, wherefore I pray to

Almighty God to give you the victory. In the matter of beginning the war at Calais, I have sent instructions to start it, and have today had certain news that the garrison of Calais had already begun and has advanced from Ardes, and has killed two of the garrison of Gravelines. As soon as I possibly can, I will come to you to serve you against this accursed Burgundian without any default, please God, to whom I pray to grant you all that your high heart desires. Written at London the 13th day of February.

(Signed) Your very humble servant,
R Warrewyk.

From (**77**), p. 115.

document 21

The Death of Henry VI, 21 May 1471

Official Yorkist Account:

. . . it appeared to every man at a glance that the said party [Lancastrians] was extinct and repressed for ever, without any kind of hope of revival. . . . The certainty of all this came to the knowledge of the said Henry, lately called king, being in the Tower of London; not having, before that, knowledge of the said matters, he took it to such great hatred, anger, and indignation, that of pure displeasure and melancholy he died the 23rd day of the month of May.

Historie of the Arrivall of King Edward IV (**10**), p. 38.

And the same night that King Edward came to London, King Harry being imprisoned in the Tower of London, was put to death, the 21st May, on a Tuesday night, between 11 and 12 o'clock, being then at the Tower the Duke of Gloucester, brother to King Edward, and many others.

John Warkworth (**23**), p. 21.

. . . for him shortly afterwards God showed sundry miracles, of whose death the common fame then went that the Duke of Gloucester was not all guiltless.

The Great Chronicle of London (**6**), p. 220.

. . . On the death of this prince diverse tales were told; but the most common fame went that he was stabbed with a dagger by the hands of the Duke of Gloucester.

Robert Fabyan (**3**), p. 662.

document 22

The Quarrel between the Dukes of Clarence and Gloucester, 1472

. . . Richard, Duke of Gloucester, sought Anne in marriage. This proposal did not suit the views of his brother, the Duke of Clarence, who had previously married the elder daughter of the earl [Warwick]. Such being the case, he caused the damsel to be concealed, in order that it might not be known by his brother where she was; as he was afraid of a division of the earl's property, which he wished to come to himself alone in right of his wife, and not to be obliged to share it with any other person. Still, however, the astuteness of the Duke of Gloucester so far prevailed that he discovered the young lady in the city of London disguised in the habit of a cookmaid; upon which he had her removed to the sanctuary of St Martin's. In consequence of this, such violent dissensions arose between the brothers and so many arguments were, with the greatest acuteness, put forward on either side, in the king's presence, who sat in judgement in the council chamber, that all present, and the lawyers even, were quite surprised that these princes should find arguments in such abundance by means of which to support their respective causes . . .

At last their most loving brother, King Edward, agreed to act as a mediator between them; and in order that the discord between princes of such high rank might not cause any hindrance to the carrying out of his royal intentions in relation to the affairs of France, the whole misunderstanding was at last set at rest, upon the following terms. The marriage of the Duke of Gloucester with Anne was to take place, and he was to have such and so much of the earl's lands as should be agreed upon between them through the mediation of arbitrators; while all the rest were to remain in the possession of the Duke of Clarence. The consequence was that little or nothing was left at the disposal of the true lady and heiress, the Countess of Warwick, to whom for the whole of her life the most noble inheritance of the Warwicks and the Despensers properly belonged.

The Croyland Chronicle (**9**), p. 557.

document 23

The Death of Clarence, February 1478

The Queen remembered the insults to her family and the calumnies with which she was reproached, namely that according to established usage she was not the legitimate wife of the king. Thus she concluded that her offspring by the king would never come to the throne, unless the duke of Clarence were removed; and of this she easily persuaded the king. The queen's alarm was intensified by the comeliness of the duke of Clarence, which would make him appear worthy of the crown: besides he possessed such mastery of popular eloquence that nothing upon which he set his heart seemed difficult for him to achieve. Accordingly whether the charge was fabricated, or a real plot revealed, the duke of Clarence was accused of conspiring the king's death by means of spells and magicians. When the charge had been considered before a court, he was condemned and put to death. The mode of execution preferred in this case was, that he should die by being plunged into a jar of sweet wine.

Dominic Mancini (**14**), pp. 63–4.

document 24

Mancini's Account of Gloucester's Usurpation, Spring 1483

On completion of the royal obsequies, and while many peers of the realm, who had received neighbouring estates, were collecting in the city, a council assembled before the arrival of the young King Edward and Richard, duke of Gloucester. In this meeting the problem of the government during the royal minority was referred to the consideration of the barons. Two opinions were propounded. One was that the duke of Gloucester should govern, because Edward in his will had so directed, and because by law the government ought to devolve on him. But this was the losing resolution; the winning was that the government should be carried on by many persons among whom the duke, far from being excluded, should be accounted the chief. . . . All who favoured the queen's family voted for this proposal, as they were afraid that, if Richard took unto himself the crown or even governed alone, they, who bore the blame of Clarence's death, would suffer death or at least be ejected from their high estate.

According to common report, the chamberlain Hastings reported all these deliberations by letter and messengers to the duke of Gloucester, because he had a friendship of long standing with the duke, and was hostile to the entire kin of the queen on account of the marquess [Dorset]. Besides, it was reported that he advised the duke to hasten to the capital with a strong force, and avenge the insult done to him by his enemies. He might easily obtain his revenge if, before reaching the city, he took the young King Edward under his protection and authority.

. . . Gloucester allied himself with the duke of Buckingham, complaining to the latter of the insult done to him by the ignoble family of the queen. Buckingham, since he was of the highest nobility, was disposed to sympathise with another noble: more especially because he had his own reasons for detesting the queen's kin: for when he was younger, he had been forced to marry the queen's sister, whom he scorned to wed on account of her humble origin.

. . . As there was current in the capital a sinister rumour that the duke had brought his nephew [Edward V] not under his care, but into his power, so as to gain himself the crown, the duke of Gloucester amidst these doings wrote to the council and the head of the city, whom they call mayor. The contents of both letters were something after this fashion. He had not confined his nephew the king of England; rather had he rescued him and the realm from perdition, since the young man would have fallen into the hands of those who, since they had not spared either the honour or life of the father, could not be expected to have more regard for the youthfulness of the son. The deed had been necessary for his own safety and to provide for that of the king and kingdom.

Having got into his power all the blood royal of the land, yet he considered that his prospects were not sufficiently secure, without the removal or imprisonment of those who had been the closest friends of his brother, and were expected to be loyal to his brother's offspring. In this class he thought to include Hastings, the king's chamberlain; Thomas Rotherham, whom shortly before he had relieved of his office: and the bishop of Ely. . . . Therefore the protector rushed headlong into crime, for fear that the ability and authority of these men might be detrimental to him. . . . One day these three and several others came to the Tower about ten o'clock to salute the protector, as was their custom. When they had been admitted to the innermost quarters, the protector, as prearranged, cried out that an ambush had been prepared for him, and they had come with hidden arms, that they might be first to open the attack. Thereupon the soldiers, who had been stationed there by their lord, rushed in with the duke of Buckingham, and cut down Hastings on the false pretext of treason; they arrested the others, whose life, it was presumed, was spared out of respect for religion and holy orders.

. . . he [Gloucester] secretly dispatched the duke of Buckingham to the lords with orders to submit to their decision the disposal of the throne. He argued that it appeared unjust that this lad, who was illegitimate, should assume the office of kingship: for he was a bastard by reason of his father Edward having married Elizabeth, when by law he was contracted to another wife, whom the duke of Warwick had given him. At Edward's [IV] command the duke had previously crossed the seas and betrothed the other lady by word of proxy, as they call it.

Dominic Mancini (**14**), pp. 71–97.

document 25

The Bishop of St Davids' opinion of Richard III in 1483

Dr Thomas Langton, Bishop of St Davids, to the Prior of Christ Church.

. . . I trust to God soon, by Michaelmas, the king shall be at London. He contents the people wherever he goes better than ever did any prince; for many a poor man that has suffered wrong many days has been relieved and helped by him and his commands in his progress. And in many great cities and towns were given to him great sums of money which he has refused. Upon my word I never liked the qualities of any prince so well as his; God has sent him to us for the weal of us all.

English Historical Documents (**16**), pp. 336–7.

document 26

Polydore Vergil on Richard III

In the mean time the body of King Richard naked of all clothing, and laid upon a horse's back with the arms and legs hanging down on both sides, was brought to the abbey of the Franciscan monks at Leicester, a miserable spectacle in good sooth, but not unworthy for the man's life, and there was buried two days after without any pomp or solemn funeral. He reigned two years and so many months, and one day over. He was little of stature, deformed of body, the one shoulder being higher than the other, a short and sour countenance, which seemed to savour of mischief, and utter evidently craft and deceit. The while he was thinking of any matter, he did continually bite his nether lip, as though that cruel nature of his did so rage against itself in that little carcase. Also he was wont to be ever with his right hand pulling out of the sheath to the middest, and putting in again, the dagger which he did always wear. Truly he had a sharp wit, provident and subtle, apt both to counterfeit and dissemble; his courage also high and fierce, which failed him not in the very death, which, when his men forsook him, he rather yielded to take with the sword, than by foul flight to prolong his life, uncertain what death perchance soon after by sickness or other violence to suffer.

Polydore Vergil (**22**), pp. 226–7.

document 27

John Rous on Richard III

The most mighty prince Richard, by the grace of God king of England and of France and lord of Ireland . . . all avarice set aside, ruled his subjects in his Realm full commendably, punishing offenders of his laws, especially extortioners and oppressors of his Commons, and cherishing those that were virtuous, by the which discreet guiding he got the great thanks of God and the love of all his subjects rich and poor and the great praise of the people of all other lands about him.

The Rous Roll (**20**), cap. 63.

Richard was born at Fotheringhay in Northamptonshire, retained within his mother's womb for two years and emerging with teeth and hair to his shoulder. . . . And like a scorpion he combined a smooth front with a stinging tail. He received his lord King Edward V blandly, with embraces and kisses, and within about three months or a little more he killed him together with his brother. And Lady Anne, his queen, daughter of the Earl of Warwick, he poisoned

. . . and what was most detestable to God and all Englishmen, indeed to all nations to whom it became known, he caused others to kill the holy man King Henry VI, or, as many think, did so by his own hands. . . . He was small of stature, with a short face and unequal shoulders, the right higher and the left lower.

Historia Regum Angliae (**19**), pp. 120–1.

document 28

The Princes in the Tower, 1483

. . . after Hastings was removed, all the attendants who had waited upon the king were debarred access to him. He and his brother were withdrawn into the inner apartments of the Tower proper, and day by day began to be seen more rarely behind the bars and windows, till at length they ceased to appear altogether. Dr Argentine, the last of his attendants whose service the king enjoyed, reported that the young king, like a victim prepared for sacrifice, sought remission of his sins by daily confession and penance, because he believed that death was facing him.

Dominic Mancini (**14**), pp. 92–3.

And during this mayor's year [Sir Edmund Shaw, who ended his mayoralty on 28 October 1483] the children of King Edward were seen shooting and playing in the garden of the Tower at sundry times. All the winter season of this mayor's time [Robert Billesdon, October 1483–October 1484] the land was in good quiet, but after Easter there was much whispering among the people that the king had put the children of King Edward to death . . .

The Great Chronicle of London (**6**), p. 234.

Item: this yer King Edward the Vth, late callyd Preince Walys, and Richard duke of Yourke hys brother, Kyng Edward the iiij sonys, wer put to deyth in the Towur of London be the vise of the duke of Buckingham.

Historical Notes of a London citizen (**65**), p. 588.

document 29
The Death of Richard III and the Council of York

King Richard, late mercifully reigning upon us, . . . with many other lords and nobility of these northern parts, was piteously slain and murdered, to the great heaviness of this city.

York Records (**26**), p. 218.

document 30
Polydore Vergil's account of the internal disorder in the Wars of the Roses

This, finally, was the end of the foreign war, and likewise the renewal of civil calamity: for when the fear of an external enemy, which had kept the kingdom in good exercise, was gone from the nobility, such was the contention amongst them for glory and power, that even then the people were apparently divided into two factions, according as it became afterwards, when those two, that is to say, king Henry, who derived his pedigree from the house of Lancaster, and Richard duke of York, who conveyed himself by his mother's side from Lionel, son of Edward the Third, contended for the kingdom. By means whereof these two factions grew shortly so great through the whole realm that, while the one sought by any manner to subdue the other, and raged in revenge upon the subdued, many men were utterly destroyed, and the whole realm brought to ruin and decay.

Polydore Vergil (**22**), pp. 93–4.

document 31
Edward IV's Speech to Parliament, 1467

The cause why I have called and summoned this my present Parliament is, that I purpose to live upon mine own, and not to charge my subjects but in great and urgent causes, concerning more the weal of themselves, and also the defence of them and of this my realm, rather than mine own pleasure, as here to fore by Commons of this land hath been done and borne unto my progenitors in time of need; wherein I trust that ye Sirs, and all the Commons of this my land will be as tender and kind unto me in such cases, as heretofore any Commons have been to any of my said progenitors.

From *Rotuli Parliamentorum*, vol. 5, p. 572.

document 32

The Financial Policies of Edward IV

. . . he bent all his thoughts to the question, how he might in future collect an amount of treasure worthy of his royal station out of his own substance, and by the exercise of his own energies. Accordingly, having called Parliament together, he resumed possession of nearly all the royal estates, without regard to whom they had been granted, and applied the whole thereof to the support of the expenses of the crown. Throughout all the ports of the kingdom he appointed surveyors of the customs, men of remarkable shrewdness, but too hard, according to general report, upon the merchants. The king himself, also, having procured merchant ships, put on board of them the finest wools, cloths, tin and other products of the kingdom, and, like a private individual living by trade, exchanged merchandise for merchandise, by means of his factors, among both Italians and Greeks. The revenues of vacant prelacies, which, according to Magna Carta, cannot be sold, he would only part with out of his hands at a stated sum, and on no other terms whatever. He also examined the register and rolls of Chancery, and exacted heavy fines from those whom he found to have intruded and taken possession of estates without prosecuting their rights in form required by law, by way of return for the rents which they had in the meantime received. These, and more of a similar nature than can possibly be conceived by a man who is inexperienced in such matters, were his methods of making up a purse; added to which, there was the yearly tribute of ten thousand pounds due from the French, together with numerous tenths from the churches, from which the prelates and clergy had been unable to get themselves excused. All these particulars, in the course of a very few years, rendered him an extremely wealthy prince.

The Croyland Chronicle (**9**), p. 559.

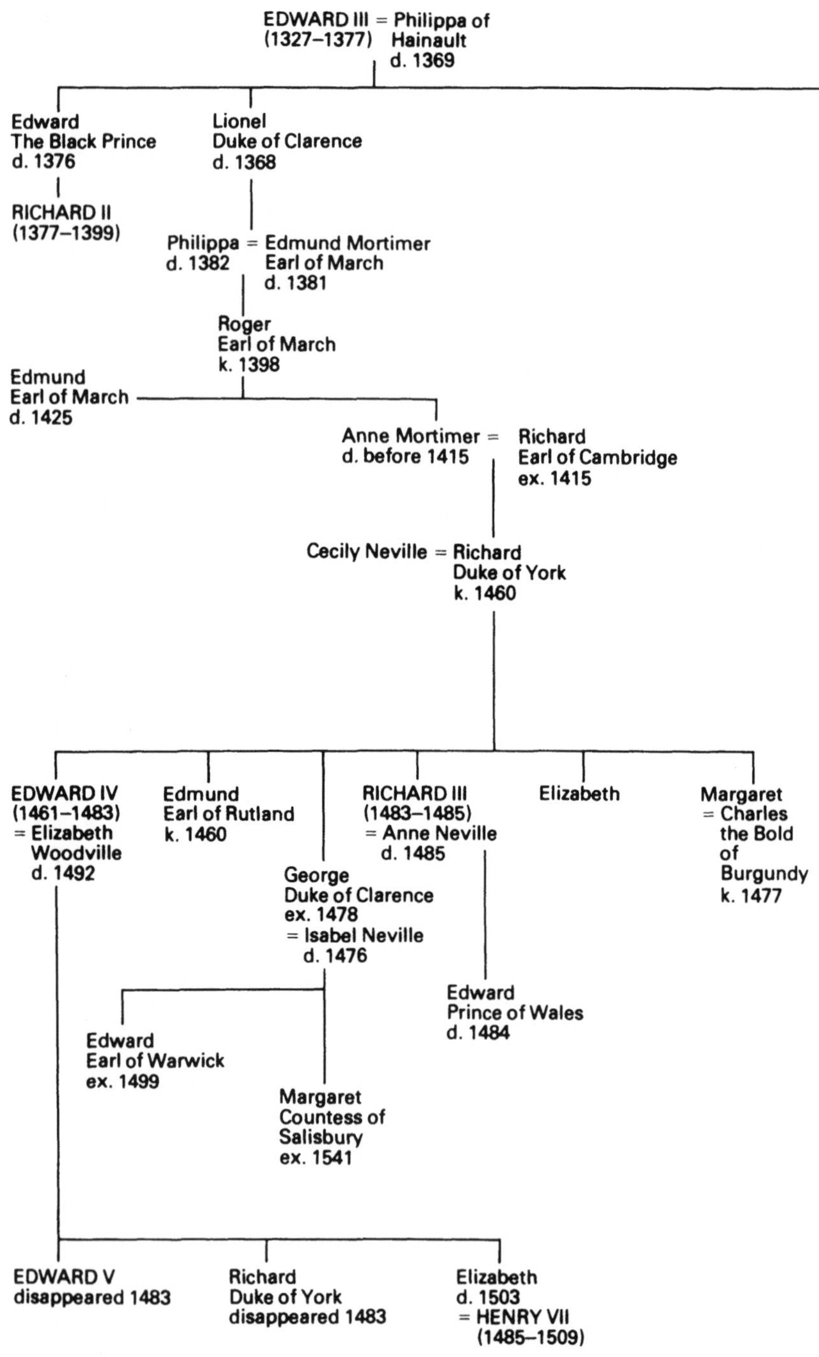
EDWARD III = Philippa of
(1327–1377) Hainault
d. 1369
Edward
The Black Prince
d. 1376
Lionel
Duke of Clarence
d. 1368
RICHARD II
(1377–1399)
Philippa = Edmund Mortimer
d. 1382 Earl of March
d. 1381
Roger
Earl of March
k. 1398
Edmund
Earl of March
d. 1425
Anne Mortimer = Richard
d. before 1415 Earl of Cambridge
ex. 1415
Cecily Neville = Richard
Duke of York
k. 1460
EDWARD IV
(1461–1483)
= Elizabeth
Woodville
d. 1492
Edmund
Earl of Rutland
k. 1460
RICHARD III
(1483–1485)
= Anne Neville
d. 1485
Elizabeth
Margaret
= Charles
the Bold
of
Burgundy
k. 1477
George
Duke of Clarence
ex. 1478
= Isabel Neville
d. 1476
Edward
Prince of Wales
d. 1484
Edward
Earl of Warwick
ex. 1499
Margaret
Countess of
Salisbury
ex. 1541
EDWARD V
disappeared 1483
Richard
Duke of York
disappeared 1483
Elizabeth
d. 1503
= HENRY VII
(1485–1509)

LANCASTER AND YORK

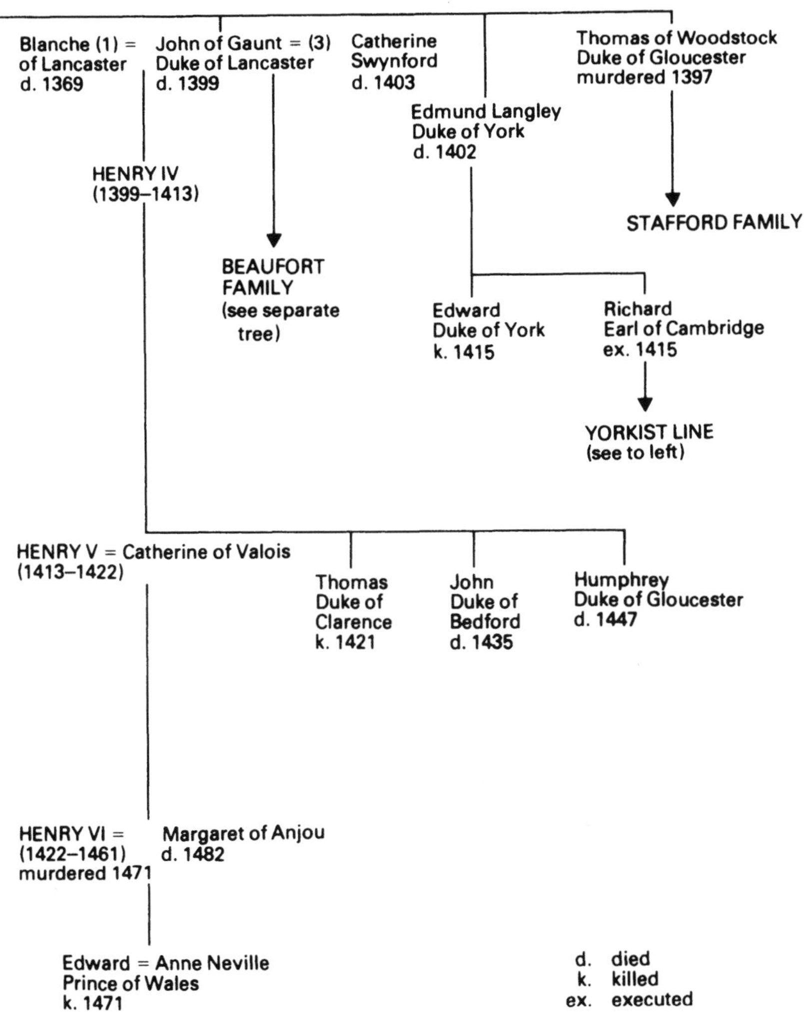

d. died
k. killed
ex. executed

BEAUFORT FAMILY

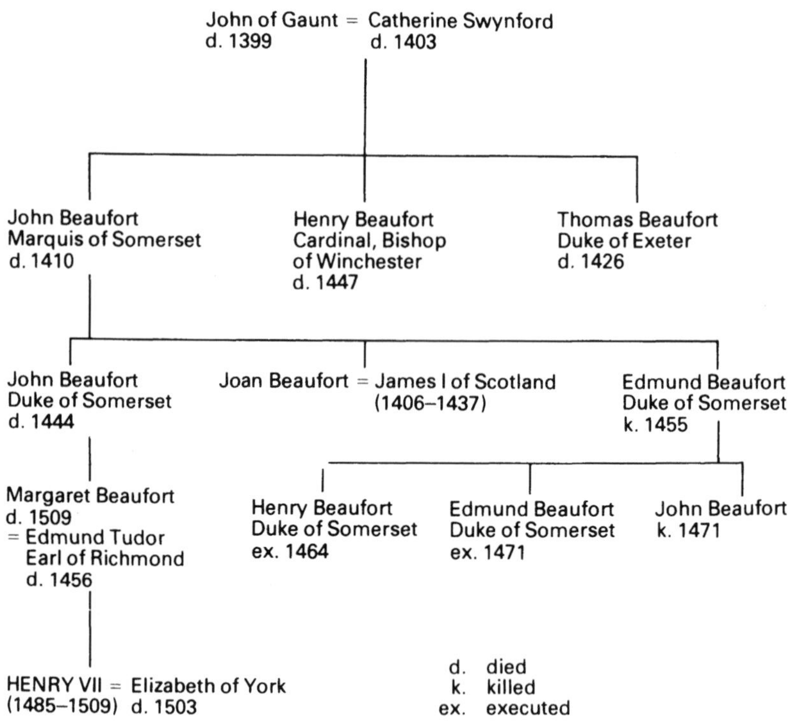

THE NEVILLES

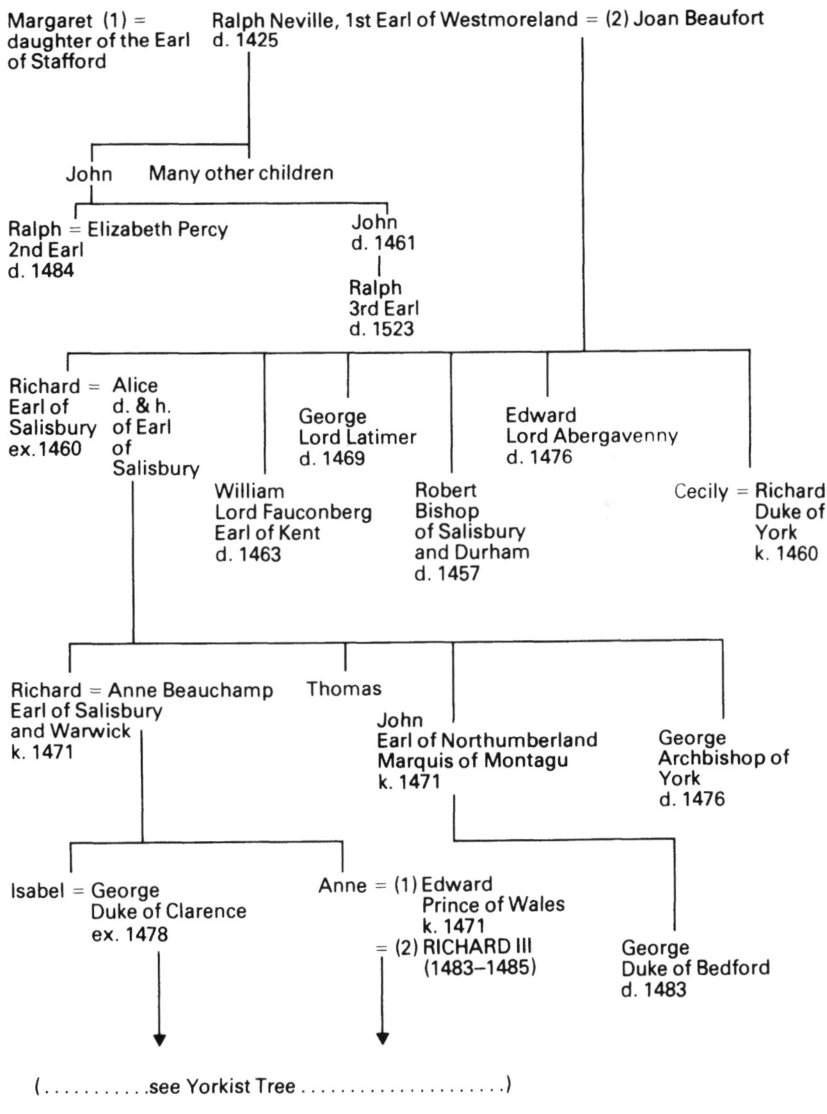

d. died
k. killed
ex. executed
d. & h. daughter and heiress

The Battles in the Wars of the Roses

1455 May: St Albans.

1459 September: Blore Heath.

1460 July: Northampton.
December: Wakefield.

1461 February: Mortimer's Cross.
February: St Albans.
March: Towton.

1464 April: Hedgeley Moor.
May: Hexham.

1469 July: Edgecote.

1470 March: 'Lose-coat Field', near Stamford.

1471 April: Barnet.
May: Tewkesbury.

1485 August: Bosworth.

1487 June: Stoke.

Glossary

(*Act of Resumption*): a parliamentary act to recover all royal lands which have been alienated.

(*Benevolences*): supposedly free 'gifts' exacted by Edward IV in lieu of military service.

(*Chevauchées*): highly destructive military campaigns, usually associated with the Black Prince in the Hundred Years War.

(*Gentry*): members of the landowning class immediately below the peerage.

(*Nobility*): peerage-holding landowning class.

(*Readeption of Henry VI*): period 1470–1 when Henry VI was restored to the English throne by the Earl of Warwick.

(*Statute of Limitations*): statute setting a date in the past, beyond which claims are no longer valid in law, in an attempt to limit conflicts over property rights.

(*Wardships*): the guardianship of an under-age heir and of his estates. In the case of tenants-in-chief the heir became a royal ward.

Bibliography

PRIMARY SOURCES

1 Commynes, Philippe de. *The Memoirs for the Reign of Louis XI, 1461–1483*, trans. by Michael Jones, Penguin Classics, 1972.

2 Davies, J. S., ed. *An English Chronicle of the Reigns of Richard II, Henry IV, Henry V and Henry VI*, Camden Society, 1856.

3 Fabyan, R. *New Chronicles of England and France*, ed. H. Ellis, London, 1811.

4 Fortescue, John. *The Governance of England*, ed. C. Plummer, Oxford University Press, 1885.

5 *Gesta Henrici Quinti*, trans. by F. Taylor and J. S. Roskell, Oxford University Press, 1975.

6 *The Great Chronicle of London*, ed. A. H. Thomas and I. D. Thornley, London, Guildhall Library, 1938.

7 Hall, Edward. *Union of the Two Illustre Families of Lancaster and York*, ed. H. Ellis, London 1809.

8 Hardyng, John. *Chronicle*, ed. H. Ellis, London, 1812 and ed. C. L. Kingsford in *English Historical Review*, XXVII, 1912.

9 'Historiae Croylandensis Continuatio', in *Rerum Anglicarum Scriptores Veterum*, ed. W. Fulman, Oxford University Press, 1684; trans. by H. T. Riley, *Ingulph's Chronicles*, London, 1854.

10 *Historie of the Arrivall of King Edward IV*, ed. J. Bruce, Camden Society, 1838.

11 Horrox, R. and Hammond, P. W. *British Library Harleian Manuscript 433*, 4 vols., Alan Sutton, 1979–

12 James, M. R., ed. *Henry the Sixth: a reprint of John Blacman's Memoir*, Cambridge University Press, 1919.

13 Kingsford, C. L., ed. *Chronicles of London*, reprinted Alan Sutton, 1977.

14 Mancini, Dominic. *The Usurpation of Richard III*, ed. C. A. J. Armstrong, 2nd edn, Oxford University Press, 1969.

15 More, Sir Thomas. *The History of King Richard III*, ed. R. S. Sylvester, Yale University Press, 1963.

16 Myers, A. R., ed. *English Historical Documents Vol. IV, 1327–1485*, Methuen, 1969.

17 *The Paston Letters, 1422–1509*, ed. James Gairdner, 6 vols., 1904; also *Paston Letters and Papers of the Fifteenth Century*, ed. N. Davis, 2 vols., Oxford University Press, 1971–1976.
18 *Rotuli Parliamentorum*, ed. J. Strachey and others, 6 vols., London, 1767–1777.
19 Rous, John. *Historia Regum Angliae*, ed. T. Hearne, Oxford University Press, 1745.
20 Rous, John. *The Rous Roll*, 1859, reprinted Alan Sutton, 1980.
21 Stevenson, J., ed. *Letters and Papers Illustrative of the Wars of the English in France during the Reign of Henry VI*, 2 vols., Rolls Series, 1861–1864.
22 Vergil, Polydore. *Three Books of Polydore Vergil's English History*, ed. H. Ellis, Camden Society, 1844.
23 Warkworth, John. *A Chronicle of the First Thirteen Years of the Reign of King Edward the Fourth*, ed. J. O. Halliwell, Camden Society, 1839.
24 Waurin, Jean de. *Recueil des Chroniques*, ed. W. and E. L. C. P. Hardy, 5 vols., Rolls Series, 1864–1891.
25 Whethamstede, John. *Registrum*, ed. H. T. Riley, 2 vols., Rolls Series, 1872–1873.
26 *York Records: Extracts from the Municipal Records of the City of York*, ed. R. Davies, London, 1843.

BOOKS AND PAMPHLETS

27 Allmand, C. T. *Henry V*, Historical Association Pamphlet G.68, 1968.
28 Bellamy, J. *Crime and Public Order in England in the Later Middle Ages*, Routledge & Kegan Paul, 1973.
29 Brooks, F. W. *The Council of the North*, Historical Association Pamphlet G. 25; rev. edn 1966.
30 Chrimes, S. B., Ross, C. D. and Griffiths, R. A., eds. *Fifteenth Century England, 1399–1509*, Manchester University Press, 1972.
31 Dunham, W. H. *Lord Hastings' Indentured Retainers*, Connecticut Academy of Arts and Sciences Transactions, 1955.
32 Gairdner, James. *History of the Life and Reign of Richard III*, Cambridge University Press, 1898.
33 Gillingham, John. *The Wars of the Roses*, Weidenfeld and Nicolson, 1981.
34 Goodman, A. *A History of England from Edward II to James I*, Longman, 1977.
35 Goodman, A. *The Wars of the Roses, Military Activity and English Society, 1452–97*, Routledge & Kegan Paul, 1981.

36 Griffiths, R. A. *The Reign of King Henry VI*, Ernest Benn, 1981.

37 Hanham, A. *Richard III and his Early Historians 1483–1535*, Clarendon Press, 1975.

38 Hay, Denys. *Polydore Vergil, Renaissance Historian and Man of Letters*, Clarendon Press, 1952.

39 Hicks, M. A. *False, Fleeting, Perjur'd Clarence: George, Duke of Clarence 1449–1478*, Alan Sutton, 1980.

40 Keen, M. H. *England in the Later Middle Ages*, Methuen, 1973.

41 Kendall, P. M. *Richard III*, Allen and Unwin, 1955.

42 Lander, J. R. *The Wars of the Roses*, Secker and Warburg, 1968.

43 Lander, J. R. *Conflict and Stability in Fifteenth-Century England*, Hutchinson, 1969.

44 Lander, J. R. *Crown and Nobility*, Edward Arnold, 1976. (This is a collection of Lander's most important articles, which have not therefore been listed separately.)

45 Lander, J. R. *Government and Community: England 1450–1509*, Edward Arnold, 1980.

46 McFarlane, K. B. 'The Lancastrian Kings', in *Cambridge Medieval History, VIII*, Cambridge University Press, 1936.

47 McFarlane, K. B. *Lancastrian Kings and Lollard Knights*, Oxford University Press, 1972.

48 McFarlane, K. B. *The Nobility of Later Medieval England*, Oxford University Press, 1973.

49 McKisack, May. *The Fourteenth Century, 1307–1399*, Oxford University Press, 1959.

50 Myers, A. R. *The Household of Edward IV*, Manchester University Press, 1959.

51 Rawcliffe, Carole. *The Staffords, Earls of Stafford and Dukes of Buckingham, 1394–1521*, Cambridge University Press, 1978.

52 Reid, R. R. *The King's Council in the North*, reprinted E.P. Group of Companies, 1975.

53 Richmond, C. F. *John Hopton: A Fifteenth-Century Suffolk Gentleman*, Cambridge University Press, 1981.

54 Ross, C. D. *Edward IV*, Eyre Methuen, 1974.

55 Ross, C. D. ed. *Patronage, Pedigree and Power in Later Medieval England*, Alan Sutton, 1979.

56 Ross, C. D. *Richard III*, Eyre Methuen, 1981.

57 Somerville, R. *History of the Duchy of Lancaster, 1265–1603*, London, 1953.

58 Storey, R. L. *The End of the House of Lancaster*, Barrie and Rockliff, 1966.

59 Wolffe, B. P. *The Crown Lands*, 1461–1536, George Allen and Unwin, 1970.

60 Wolffe, B. P. *The Royal Demesne in English History*, Allen and Unwin, 1971.

61 Wolffe, B. P. *Henry VI*, Eyre Methuen, 1981.

ARTICLES AND ESSAYS

The following abbreviations are used:

BIHR	*Bulletin of the Institute of Historical Research*
BJRL	*Bulletin of the John Rylands Library*
EHR	*English Historical Review*
JMH	*Journal of Medieval History*
PPP	*Patronage, Pedigree and Power in Later Medieval England*, ed. C. D. Ross, 1979, (**55**).
TRHS	*Transactions of the Royal Historical Society*

62 Armstrong, C. A. J. 'Politics and the battle of St Albans, 1455', *BIHR*, 33 (1960).

63 Carpenter, C. 'The Beauchamp affinity: a study of bastard feudalism at work', *EHR*, 95 (1980).

64 Coleman, C. H. D. 'The execution of Hastings: a neglected source', *BIHR*, 53 (1980).

65 Green, R. F. 'Historical notes of a London citizen, 1483–1488' *EHR*, 96 (1981).

66 Griffiths, R. A. 'Local rivalries and national politics: the Percies, the Nevilles and the Duke of Exeter', *Speculum*, 43 (1968).

67 Griffiths, R. A. 'The trial of Eleanor Cobham: an episode in the fall of Duke Humphrey of Gloucester', *BJRL*, 51 (1968–9).

68 Griffiths, R. A. 'Duke Richard of York's intentions in 1450 and the origins of the Wars of the Roses', *JMH*, 1, (1975).

69 Griffiths, R. A. 'The sense of dynasty in the reign of Henry VI', *PPP*.

70 Hanham, A. 'Richard III, Lord Hastings and the historians', *EHR*, 88 (1972).

71 Hanham, A. 'Hastings Redivivus', *EHR*, 90 (1975).

72 Harriss, G. L. 'The struggle for Calais: an aspect of the rivalry between Lancaster and York', *EHR*, 75 (1960).

73 Harriss, G. L. 'Cardinal Beaufort: patriot or usurer?' *TRHS* (5th series), 20 (1970).

74 Hicks, M. A. 'The changing role of the Wydevilles in Yorkist politics to 1483', *PPP*.

75 McFarlane, K. B. 'Parliament and bastard feudalism,' *TRHS* (4th Series), 26 (1944).
76 McFarlane, K. B. 'The Wars of the Roses', *Proceedings of the British Academy*, 50 (1964).
77 Myers, A. R. 'The outbreak of war between England and Burgundy in February 1471', *BIHR*, 23 (1960).
78 Myers, A. R. 'Richard III and historical tradition', *History*, 53 (1968).
79 Pollard, A. J. 'The tyranny of Richard III', *JMH*, 3 (1977).
80 Pollard, A. J. 'The Richmondshire community of gentry during the Wars of the Roses', *PPP*.
81 Pugh, T. B. 'The magnates, knights and gentry', in *Fifteenth-Century England*, ed. Chrimes and others (1972), no. 30.
82 Roskell, J. S. 'The problem of the attendance of the Lords in medieval parliaments', *BIHR*, 39 (1956).
83 Ross, C. D. 'The estates and finances of Richard, Duke of York', *Welsh History Review*, 3 (1967).
84 Storey, R. L. 'The Wardens of the Marches of England towards Scotland, 1377–1489', *EHR*, 72 (1957).
85 Sutton, A. F. and Hammond, P. W. 'The problems of dating and the dangers of redating', *Journal of Society of Archivists*, 6 (1978).
86 Thomson, J. A. F. 'Richard III and Lord Hastings – a problematical case reviewed', *BIHR*, 48 (1975).
87 Virgoe, R. 'The death of William de la Pole, Duke of Suffolk', *BJRL*, 47 (1965).
88 Wolffe, B. P. 'When and why did Hastings lose his head?' *EHR*, 89 (1974).
89 Wolffe, B. P. 'Hastings reinterred', *EHR*, 91 (1976).
90 Wood, Charles T. 'The deposition of Edward V', *Traditio*, 31 (1975).

Index